Contemporary's Whole Language Series

NONFICTION SELECTIONS

Contemporary's Whole Language Series

VIEWPOINTS

NONFICTION SELECTIONS

VOLUME 2

Pat Fiene
Project Editor

Ted Knight
Research and Development

CB

CONTEMPORARY BOOKS

a division of NTC/CONTEMPORARY PUBLISHING GROUP
Lincolnwood, Illinois USA

Library of Congress Cataloging-in-Publication Data
(Revised for vol. 2)

Viewpoints.

   (Contemporary's whole language series)
   Vol. 2 project editor: Pat Fiene.
   1. Readers for new literates.   I. Black
Hawk, Sauk chief, 1767–1838.   II. Niemet,
Cathy.   III. Fiene, Pat.
PE1126.A4V54   1991   428.6′2   91-20924
ISBN 0-8092-3647-8

Photo Credits
The Stock Market: page viii © Jeffry Meyers; page 28 © Joe Sohm/
Chromosohm, 1989; page 50 © Mugshots 1992; page 74 ©
DiMaggio/Kalish 1988; page 108 © Richard Dunoff; page 130 ©
Richard Steedman 1989. Retna. Ltd.: page 90 © John Atashian.

ISBN: 0-8092-3647-8

Published by Contemporary Books,
a division of NTC/Contemporary Publishing Group, Inc.,
4255 West Touhy Avenue,
Lincolnwood (Chicago), Illinois 60646-1975 U.S.A.
© 1994 by NTC/Contemporary Publishing Group, Inc.
Manufactured in the United States of America.

   8 9 0 HAM HAM 0 9 8 7 6 5 4 3

Editorial Director
Mark Boone

Editorial
Craig Bolt
Lisa Dillman
Ann Wambach

Editorial Production Manager
Norma Underwood

Cover Design
Georgene Sainati

Cover Illustrator
Kathy Petrauskas

Photo Researcher
Steven Diamond

Typography
Terrence Alan Stone

TO THE READER

Welcome to *Viewpoints, Volume 2*. Thumb through this book. No matter what subjects you enjoy reading about, you're bound to find a theme that captures your interest.

Are you touched by stories about people who care? Then you'll want to read the articles in Sons and Daughters and Acts of Kindness and Love.

If harder-edged stories about real-life problems are more your style, try Short Lives, Hard Lives. The articles in this unit will make you angry—and sad.

Read about the problems of newcomers to the United States in Caught Between Cultures. Learn the interesting stories behind four everyday things in Where Did It Come From? Celebrate the human spirit in Turning Points and Trading Places.

After you finish a reading, take time out to reflect and write. Draw on your own experiences to understand the experiences you read about. On your way to understanding them, you will come to understand more about yourself.

We hope that you enjoy *Viewpoints, Volume 2*.

The Editors

CONTENTS

SONS AND DAUGHTERS   1

Lost in America   *Dave Barry*   2

*From·*The Parrot's Beak   *Kartar Dhillon*   6

Friend or Father?   *Anthony Walton*   10

In Search of Eels   *Elisavietta Ritchie*   17

CAUGHT BETWEEN CULTURES   29

Around Brick Walls   *Sarah Delany*   30

Fitting In   *S. Beth Atkin*   34

Interview with Adam Hryniewicki
    Mary Motley Kalergis   40

For My Indian Daughter   *Lewis Sawaquat*   42

ACTS OF KINDNESS AND LOVE   51

Above and Beyond   *Bob Greene*   52

The Good Stuff   *Robert Fulghum*   56

Grandma Hattie   *Tom Bodett*   61

The Overspill   *Fred Chappell*   65

WHERE DID IT COME FROM?   75

The Shopping Cart   *Vince Staten*   76

Chewing Gum   *Don L. Wulffson*   79

Velcro: Improving on Nature   *Ira Flatow*   82

Dr. Pemberton's Pick-Me-Up   *Paul Aurandt*   85

TURNING POINTS 91

Words in a Blue Notebook *Eula Lee Maddox* 92

From Freedom *Charlotte Painter* 95

And I Never Did *Louie Anderson* 97

From Me and the Guy Upstairs
  Penny Longworth 101

TRADING PLACES 109

Wednesday, February 28 *John Coleman* 110

From Linen Bliss *Teresa Jordan* 113

Hispanic, USA: The Conveyor Belt Ladies
  Rose Del Castillo Guilbault 120

From Workers *Richard Rodriguez* 126

SHORT LIVES, HARD LIVES 131

From A Tragedy Too Easy to Ignore *Mitch Albom* 132

Children's Fears *Nicholas Duva* 137

To Defray Expenses *Anna Quindlen* 139

January 9, 1991 *Latoya Hunter* 143

Fear *Gary Soto* 144

Note to the Instructor: The teacher's guide contains a step-by-step lesson plan and activities for every theme.

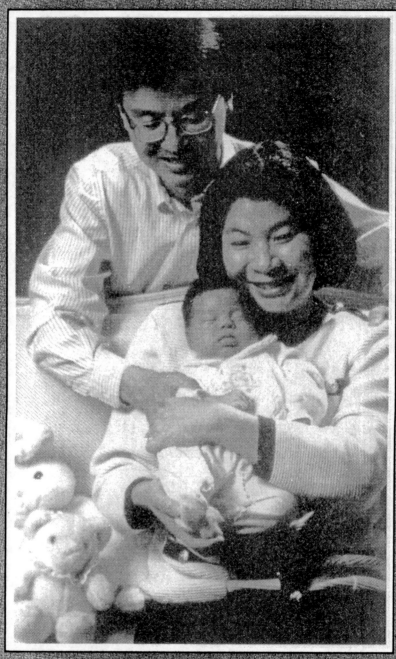

New parents hold up their baby daughter for the camera. Their shy grins show the pride and love they feel.

SONS AND DAUGHTERS

How does the relationship between a parent and child change when the child becomes an adult? Has your relationship with a parent or guardian changed as you have become older? How do you think it might change in the future?

The relationship between parents and children is an important one. Usually, however, we focus on the period when the children are young and under the care of their parents. We don't talk as much about the kinds of relationships that exist between parents and their grown children, even though these relationships may last much longer than only eighteen or twenty-one years.

As the following readings show, relationships between parents and their adult children vary. Sometimes the relationship stays about the same as it was when the child was young. Sometimes it changes and keeps changing. Sometimes the roles even become reversed, as aging parents become dependent upon their children.

As you read, think about your experiences as a son or a daughter. How are they similar to the experiences of the writers in this unit? How are they different?

*Award-winning newspaper columnist
Dave Barry usually writes funny stories
about current events. But in the following column, Barry writes about a serious
subject—his mother's unhappiness after
her husband's death. Many of us will
find ourselves trying to help a recently
widowed parent build a new life.*

Lost in America

In *Dave Barry Turns 40*
Dave Barry

My mother and I are driving through Hartford, Connecticut, on the way to a town called Essex. Neither
of us has ever been to Essex, but we're both desperately hoping that my mother will want to live there.

She has been rootless for several months now,
moving from son to son around the country, ever
since she sold the house she had lived in for forty
years, the house she raised us in, the house my father
built. The house where he died, April 4, 1984. She
would note the date each year on the calendar in the
kitchen.

"Dave died, 1984," the note would say. "Come
back, Dave."

The note for July 5, their anniversary, said:
"Married Dave, 1942. Best thing that ever happened
to me."

The house was too big for my mother to handle
alone, and we all advised her to sell it. Finally she
did, and she shipped all her furniture to Sunnyvale,
California, where my brother Phil lived. Her plan was
to stay with him until she found a place of her own
out there.

Only she hated Sunnyvale. At first this seemed almost funny, even to her. "All my worldly goods," she would say, marveling[1] at it, "are in a warehouse in Sunnyvale, California, which I hate." She always had a wonderful sense of absurdity.[2]

After a while it didn't seem so funny. My mother left Sunnyvale to live for a while with my brother Sam, in San Francisco, and then with me, in Florida; but she didn't want to stay with us. What she wanted was a home.

What she really wanted was her old house back.

With my father in it.

Of course, she knew she couldn't have that, but when she tried to think of what else she wanted, her mind would just lock up. She started to spend a lot of time watching soap operas. "You have to get on with your life," I would tell her, in this new, parental voice I was developing when I talked to her. Dutifully,[3] she would turn off the TV and get out a map of the United States, which I bought her to help her think.

"Maybe Boulder would be nice," she would say, looking at Colorado. "I was born near Boulder."

"Mom," I would say in my new voice. "We've talked about Boulder fifty times, and you always end up saying you don't really want to live there."

Chastened,[4] she would look back at her map, but I could tell she wasn't really seeing it.

"You have to be realistic," I would say. The voice of wisdom.

When she and I had driven each other just about crazy, she went back out to California, and repeated the process with both of my brothers. Then one night

---

[1] marveling: feeling amazed
[2] absurdity: foolishness
[3] dutifully: with a sense of duty; obediently
[4] chastened: shamed

she called to ask, very apologetically,⁵ if I would go with her to look at Essex, Connecticut, which she had heard was nice. It was a bad time for me, but of course I said yes, because your mom is your mom. I met her in Hartford and rented a car.

* * *

I'm driving; my mother is looking out the window. "I came through Hartford last year with Frank and Mil, on the way to Maine," she says. Frank was my father's brother; he has just died. My mother loved to see him. He reminded her of my father.

"We were singing," my mother says. She starts to sing:

"I'm forever blowing bubbles
Pretty bubbles in the air."

I can tell she wants me to sing, too. I know the words; we sang this song when I was little.

"First they fly so high, nearly reach the sky
Then like my dreams, they fade and die."

But I don't sing. I am all business.
"I miss Frank," says my mother.
Essex turns out to be a beautiful little town, and we look at two nice, affordable apartments. But I can tell right away that my mother doesn't want to be there. She doesn't want to say so, after asking me to fly up from Miami, but we both know.
The next morning, in the motel coffee shop, we have a very tense breakfast.
"Look, Mom," I say, "you have to make some kind of decision." Sounding very reasonable.
She looks down at her map. She starts talking about Boulder again. This sets me off. I lecture⁶ her,

---

⁵apologetically: with apology; regretfully
⁶lecture: criticize

tell her she's being childish. She's looking down at her map, gripping it. I drive her back to Hartford, neither of us saying much. I put her on a plane; she's going to Milwaukee, to visit my dad's sister, then back to my brother in Sunnyvale, California. Which she hates.

The truth is, I'm relieved that she's leaving.

"You can't help her," I tell myself, "until she decides what she wants." It is a sound[7] position.

About a week later, my wife and I get a card from my mother.

"This is to say happy birthday this very special year," it says. "And to thank you for everything."

Our birthdays are weeks away.

About two days later, my brother Phil calls, crying, from a hospital. My mother has taken a massive[8] overdose of Valium and alcohol. The doctors want permission to turn off the machines. They say there's no hope.

We talk about it, but there really isn't much to say. We give the permission.

It's the only logical choice.

The last thing I saw my mother do, just before she went down the tunnel to her plane, was turn and give me a big smile. It wasn't a smile of happiness; it was the same smile I give my son when he gets upset listening to the news, and I tell him don't worry, we're never going to have a nuclear war.

I can still see that smile anytime I want. Close my eyes, and there it is. A mom, trying to reassure her boy that everything's going to be okay.

---

[7] sound: sensible
[8] massive: huge

Kartar Dhillon's parents came to this country from India. The views about child rearing that they brought with them clashed with American ways, causing difficulty for their three daughters. In this reading, Dhillon describes how, at the age of sixteen, she learned how deeply her mother cared for her.

from *The Parrot's Beak*

In *Making Waves*
Kartar Dhillon

My mother was sure she would die after surgery. A doctor told her she would have to go to the county hospital in Fresno to have a tumor removed. Her first sight of the doctor in the hospital confirmed[1] her fears.

"That man does not like Indians," she told us. "He is the one who let Labh Singh die."

She had never been a patient in a hospital. Her eight children had been born at home with the help of midwives.[2] The day before entering the hospital she lay in her bed and brooded[3] about the fate of her children. She was forty-one years old, widowed for five years. Her youngest child, born after the death of our father, was five years old, and her first-born, delivered a few weeks after her arrival in the United States in 1910, was twenty-one. Her husband had promised his brother in India that his first-born son would be his son because he had no children of his

---

[1] confirmed: supported
[2] midwives: people who assist women in childbirth
[3] brooded: worried deeply

own. So they taught their first-born to call them "uncle" and "aunt," which he did, and the other children, all seven of us, hearing these terms, called our father and mother uncle and aunt also. "Chacha" and "Chachi" were our names for them, uncle and aunt on the father's side.

My parents had five sons and three daughters, and it was the daughters who worried our mother the most. Whatever we did that was different from the proper behavior of young girls in her village in India signified[4] danger. And because most things here were different, I was in constant trouble.

At a very early age, I became convinced that my mother hated me. It seemed to me that whatever I did, or didn't do, was wrong. She cursed and beat me so much that I automatically ducked if she lifted her hand. When entering a room, I kept to the edges to stay out of her arm's reach.

"Get up, you black-faced witch," was a usual eye-opener for me in the morning. And throughout the day, it was, "You parrot's beak," to remind me of my long, ugly nose.

Sometimes when I was no more than six or seven years old, I would wonder why she hated me so much. Watching her nurse the newest baby, I would wonder what she felt about having carried me in her body.

She frequently talked to us about God. "He made parents to be as God over their children," she explained once. "If children do not obey their parents, they will surely go to hell after they die." Hell was a place, she said, where the disobedient would have to pass through walls set so close together it

---

[4] signified: was a sign of

would be almost impossible to squeeze through them, and she would indicate a tiny space with her thumb and forefinger. I wasn't able to envision⁵ my soul, so I suffered endlessly imagining my body trying to squeeze through that tiny space.

Sometimes when she was particularly exasperated⁶ with me, she would say, "God must have given you to me to punish me for something I did in my previous life."

I went about feeling guilty most of the time, but I was never sure what I had done wrong. In time, I decided my crime was being a girl.

One day before she entered the hospital, she summoned⁷ me to her bedside, like a sovereign⁸ might summon a serf.⁹ I entered her room braced for a scolding. I knew she wouldn't hit me, because as I had grown older—I was sixteen then—she had given up on physical punishment, saying, "You are too old for whippings now. I can only appeal to your reason." The truth was, I had grown a head taller than my mother; I was too big.

I had learned long before not to speak when she scolded me for something. If I ever dared to protest an unjust accusation,¹⁰ she shouted, "Do not speak back to your elders."

At first I did not speak back because of her order; later I found not speaking to be a useful form of resistance. I would stand mute¹¹ before her at times, even when being questioned, which added to her rage and frustration.

---

⁵envision: picture
⁶exasperated: frustrated
⁷summoned: called
⁸sovereign: dictator; lord
⁹serf: slave
¹⁰unjust accusation: unfair charge against
¹¹mute: silent

I went to her bedroom that day, tall and gangly,[12] head hanging, waiting for an outpouring of abuse. But it did not come. Instead she said, "You probably know that I don't expect to come out of the hospital alive. You will be alone now, with neither father nor mother to guide you."

She had never spoken to me in a confiding[13] manner before. I felt a rush of sorrow for her, this frail[14] woman lying before me out of whose body I had come, and I felt guiltier than ever. Two days earlier she had paid a doctor in Merced with chickens, eggs, and vegetables, to learn that her tumor, grown to the size of a melon, had to be surgically removed.

"Your father wanted to arrange marriages for you and your sisters before he died," she continued, "but I absolutely refused. I told him, 'We came to this country to give our children an education. What good will it do them if they have to marry men they do not know and perhaps might not like?' You were only eleven years old when he died, you know."

"Oh yes, Chachi," I wanted to cry out to her, "I know. How well I know. But I thought it was only he who cared about me; it was only he who was kind to me. He would stop you from beating me, and when you pointed out my faults, he would say, she will learn better when she gets older, and you would reply, I doubt it. And yet it was you who saved me from a commitment I would have hated." I wanted to pour out words of gratitude, I wanted to comfort her, but I was too confused to say anything, and I remained silent.

---

[12]gangly: awkwardly lanky
[13]confiding: trusting
[14]frail: weak

Sons learn important lessons about how to be adults by watching their fathers. In the following piece, Anthony Walton describes lessons he learned from his father, Claude. One of the lessons Walton learned is that a father and son may view their relationship differently.

Friend or Father?

In *Sons on Fathers*
Anthony Walton

"You can get by, but you can't get away." I kept hearing my father's voice, and it was annoying. Here I was, spending a beautiful Saturday morning in a Santa Monica hardware store instead of driving up the California coast or sleeping in.

I was sorting through aisles of plastic pipe connectors, all because someone had tried to get away with building a sprinkler system on the cheap. The system had ruptured,[1] flooding my friend's yard and sidewalk. To avoid a hefty[2] plumber's fee, we had to do the repairs ourselves. I couldn't help hearing my father again: *"Do it right the first time."*

I've grown accustomed to hearing Claude's voice. As I've gotten older, I hear him almost every day, *"You're penny-wise and dollar-foolish." "You got champagne tastes, but a water pocket." "Don't believe everything you hear."* As my friends and I run into brick walls working our way into adulthood, I am

---

[1] ruptured: split open
[2] hefty: large

increasingly amazed at the sometimes brutal truth that my father has imparted[3] in his seemingly offhand[4] way.

One Christmas Eve, he and I were working on the furnace of a rental house he owns. It was about twenty below outside and, I thought, colder inside. Tormented by visions of a family-room fire, cocoa and pampering by my mother (I was home from college), I wanted my father to call it a day and get on with the festivities. After all, it *was* Christmas.

"We can't," said my father. "This is these people's home. They should be home on Christmas." He continued wrenching and whanging on a pipe.

I saw an opening. "Exactly. *We* should be home on Christmas."

He shook his head. "It ain't that simple."

"It'd be simple to call somebody."

"You got a thousand dollars?"

"No. But you do."

"The reason I got it is, I don't give it away on things I can do myself."

A couple of hours later, when we had finished and were loading our tools into the car, he looked at me. "See? That wasn't so hard. But nobody can tell you nothing. That thousand dollars will come in handy. In fact, I'll probably have to send it to *you*." He shook his head, closed the trunk and said, "Boy, just keep on living."

"Just keep on living." I often thought it sounded like a threat, but now I see that he was challenging me to see the world as it is and to live in it responsibly. I was like a lot of kids I knew, middle-class, happy, successful at most of what I attempted—but

---

[3] imparted: passed on
[4] offhand: casual

largely at the expense (literally) of my father and the world he created. Now as I contemplate[5] creating a world for his grandchildren, I gain more respect for such an accomplishment and the unblinking steadiness it takes.

My father is the kind of man overlooked or ridiculed[6] by the media.[7] His values—fidelity,[8] simplicity and frugality[9]—are spurned[10] by younger people, but I am beginning to see that these are the very values that keep a society functioning.

"Boy, you got to get a routine." He has gone to a job he does not like, in a steel factory, for thirty-six years. One day I asked him why, and he looked at me as if I had rocks in my head: "That's where the money is." And he has been married to the same woman for thirty-one years. "Marriage gives you a reason to do things."

As I gain more experience in a world where, it seems, virtually everything is disposable, I begin to appreciate the unsurpassed[11] values of steadiness and limited objectives. I'm reminded of the television comedy "All in the Family," and how much of the humor was directed at the willfully uninformed,[12] purposely contrary[13] Archie Bunker. It occurs to me, as I contemplate buying my first house, that everyone else, including his son-in-law, Meathead, who gloried in putting Archie down, was sleeping in Archie's house and eating Archie's grub. I'm increasingly

---

[5]contemplate: think about
[6]ridiculed: made fun of
[7]media: newspapers, TV, radio
[8]fidelity: faithfulness; loyalty
[9]frugality: thriftiness
[10]spurned: rejected
[11]unsurpassed: never improved upon
[12]willfully uninformed: stubbornly ignorant
[13]contrary: hard to get along with

aware of how much security my father has brought my adventures.

They were adventures he rarely understood. My father was born into excruciating[14] poverty in rural Mississippi during the Depression. He had very little formal education, leaving school early to support his brother and sisters, and bounced from Holly Springs, Miss., to Memphis to Chicago to the Air Force. But along the way he acquired a world view as logical as Newton's.[15]

The first and most important law of the world according to Claude is *"Have the facts."* God is the only thing he takes on faith. Recently, searching for a new lawn tractor, he went to three different dealers and got three different prices for the same machine. *"I'm from just outside Missouri; you got to show me."* He then went to a fourth dealer and purchased a larger tractor for less money.

I used to laugh at one of his hobbies, analyzing financial tables. He would look up from half an hour of calculating and announce: "Did you know if you put five cents in the bank when Columbus came to America, at 5¼ interest compounded daily, today you'd have $1,000,565,162 (or some such figure)?" Now I phone him for advice about financing a house or a car, and I'm beginning to understand how he can own real estate and several cars, educate his kids and regularly bail those kids out of jams. *"Boy, a nickel only goes so many ways. But nobody can tell you nothing. Just keep on living."*

And I've kept on living, and surrendered a lot of illusions, one by one. Claude says, *"You reap what you sow."* I call this idea karma, that what goes

---

[14]excruciating: deeply painful
[15]Newton's: Sir Isaac Newton (1642–1727), English scientist

around comes around. Claude cautioned me one night as I went out to break off with a girlfriend, "Remember, you got a sister." The notion that there was a link between my behavior and how I could expect my sister to be treated has served as a painfully clear guide ever since. And, in the current romantic and sexual climate, I like to think it's saved me some trouble. *"You can get by, but you can't get away."*

Claude values experience. I remember going with him in search of a family attorney. He decided against several without saying why, before suddenly settling on a firm right there in the office. On the way home he explained: "I was looking for a 'Daddy' kind of man. Somebody who's been through some battles, who's raised children. He had those pictures up of his grandchildren. That tells me what he values. And I think he's already made most of his mistakes." When I asked him where he had acquired all this insight he laughed. "I didn't get to be fifty and black by being stupid. You go around enough times, you begin to catch on."

Claude doesn't put a lot of stock in what he calls book learning. He says, "College never made anybody smart." But he has financed about $100,000 worth of book learning—and endured its being thrown in his face until the thrower had to return, hat in hand, for one kind of aid or another.

This leads to another basic law: *"Be realistic."* Claude sees the world very clearly, and what he sees is often not pretty. "It was like this when I got here, and it's going to be like this when I leave, so I'm not going to worry about it." I'm coming to see the wisdom in this. Young people often have to experience the world for many years before they have a hint of understanding human nature and, more important, history. For this reason, they often misread the world.

They do not understand that poverty, war and racism have always been conditions of human life. Worse, when confronted by[16] the unrelenting intractability[17] of these problems, they often abandon smaller, but equally worthy, goals.

Claude likes to say, *"If everybody would clean up his yard, the rest of the world would take care of itself."* That statement verges[18] on oversimplification, but as a way of recognizing one's true responsibilities in the world it makes irreproachable[19] sense.

This is probably the key to the world according to Claude—the power of limited objectives. By being realistic about our goals, we increase our chances of success in the long run. "Anything we do is going to be hard, and if it isn't hard, it's going to be difficult. But that just means it's going to take us a little longer." To me, this acceptance of the world and life as they are, and not as we would have them be, is the key to becoming an adult.

And so I am forced to acknowledge that the world according to Claude is increasingly, in my experience, the world as it is. I realize you *can't* put a price on a clear conscience, as Claude loves to say; very often the ability to live with one's self is all one can hope for. I'm beginning to see the power in, to spin a metaphor,[20] not needing to play every single golf course on the planet; Claude has built a putting green in his back yard and mastered that. He has made his peace with the world, and that is enough.

---

[16] confronted by: faced with
[17] unrelenting intractability: never-ending stubbornness
[18] verges: borders
[19] irreproachable: beyond criticism
[20] to spin a metaphor: to make a comparison

Most of all, I realize that every time Claude said, *"Nobody can tell you nothing,"* he went ahead and told me something—and it was always the truth. Except maybe once. We were arguing, and I took exception to what I perceived[21] as high-handedness.[22] "You should respect me," I said. "We're supposed to be friends."

He looked at me gravely. "We are not *friends.* I am your father."

I haven't quite figured this out, because he is far from being my best friend. Sometimes I'm not sure we even know each other. But it seems he is the truest friend I have had, and can expect to have.

---

[21] perceived: interpreted
[22] high-handedness: arrogance

It can be painful to have a parent living in a nursing home. In the following reading, Elisavietta Ritchie recalls a happy moment she and her elderly father experienced on an outing away from the nursing home where he lived.

In Search of Eels

In *The Tie That Binds*
Elisavietta Ritchie

"Hi, Daddy, let's take a walk."

It's a June day in Virginia. My father puts his hands on the arms of his wheelchair, whispers something I can't understand. I try to help him up but he is limp, resistant, heavy.

"Come for a walk, Daddy. Please."

The breeze billows[1] white curtains into the room. The lawns have just been mowed and the fragrance of grass wafts[2] inside.

He shivers, murmurs something about blizzards. Then, slightly more audibly,[3] "It's cold, I'm tired. Can't we go home now?"

Suddenly we're far beyond Lake Shore Drive, in a part of the waterfront I've never seen before. December, Chicago, I'm five, and cold. One mitten's lost. My feet are tired. His legs are longer, he walks too quickly through yellowing snow, gritty slush,

---

[1] billows: causes to swell
[2] wafts: is carried on a breeze
[3] audibly: loud enough to be heard

toward buildings like airplane hangars with cavernous[4] mouths. Menacing.[5]

He begins to tell me about ships and cargoes.[6]

Usually I love to listen to his stories; he knows about everything in the world. But I've had enough walking. "I want to go home."

"Just as far as that warehouse." He strides on. "Right foot, left foot, you'll see—we could hike around the whole of Lake Michigan. Come on, hold my hand—*Forward, march!*"

"I don't want to hike around Lake Michigan."

But we reach the warehouse, shed he calls it, though it is 100 times bigger than any shed in anyone's back yard. By the pier beyond are big boats: tugs and freighters and tankers and tramps. Huge anchors. I keep hoping someone will drop them with a splash into the water. But the ships are docked with thick hawsers,[7] nooses to choke the pilings.[8] Funnels and cranes. Crates taller than my father sit on the wharves. Sunday and no one is working.

Suddenly the nearest freighter bellows[9] from her funnel and I jump. From excitement, I insist, not fear.

This is the most exciting place I have ever been. I could walk along here forever. At least until I find out how to get aboard one of the boats.

Smaller sheds now, smaller boats, a green diner. Odor of fish, and smoke. We enter a shack. Barrels of brine,[10] string bags of clams, crates of fish laid out on ice, their eyes terribly wide.

"Daddy, look at that snake!"

---

[4]cavernous: cavelike
[5]menacing: threatening
[6]cargoes: goods carried on a ship
[7]hawsers: ropes used to tie boats to docks
[8]pilings: columns
[9]bellows: roars
[10]brine: very salty water

"No, that's an eel," says Daddy. "Smoked. We'll take a chunk home for supper."

"*I* certainly won't eat that!"

"All right," he says, and carries the smelly package. As we walk back, he tells me about migrations of eels to the Sargasso Sea:[11] how eels come down Dalmatian rivers and swim across the Mediterranean and then the whole Atlantic, and eels come from the rivers of North America, too, until they reach the warm Sargasso Sea. Here they spawn,[12] though I'm not quite sure what spawn means. Then the baby elvers swim back to the native rivers of their parent eels. My father explains that spawn is the proper word for something my grandmothers say people aren't supposed to discuss. But about eels, that's okay.

"Someday I will take one of these big ships. No," I correct myself, "a real ship with sails—and steer it to the Sargasso Sea."

He warns me that in the Sargasso Sea, the rudder, or the propeller screw, might get stuck in seines[13] of floating algae.[14] I'd never get home again.

Home is already far, Lake Michigan is too large, and although he sings old army marching songs to urge me to pick up my steps, toward the end of the journey he lets me ride home on his shoulders.

Back at last in the apartment, he unwraps the eel, opens his Swiss Army penknife (though he could have used the big kitchen knife) and slices carefully.

"I won't eat it," I say firmly.

"Try one bite, just for me."

"I won't like it."

---

[11]Sargasso Sea: body of water surrounding the Bermuda Islands

[12]spawn: deposit eggs

[13]seines: nets

[14]algae: water plants

While he hangs up our coats, finally I test one crumb. Awfully smelly, smokey, and salty.

He goes into the kitchen to heat milk for my cocoa, and tea for himself in the samovar[15] from Tula.[16] I test one more sliver. Then another.

He returns with the steaming cups. The eel is gone.

Because it is Sunday and I am five, he forgives me.

*   *   *

Later, I am seven, or twelve, or fifteen. We are walking along the canal, or a river, or best of all, a beach. I mostly keep up. No eels now, but we see frogs and ducks, water snakes, minnows. He tells me about everything in the world. We talk about fishing.

Sometimes at the ocean we cast from a rock or pier or the beach, though it is always the wrong bait or wrong tide. Or we drop handlines over the side of somebody's boat. On rare occasions, we catch a keeper. Then he takes out his Swiss Army knife and teaches me to gut, clean, and filet. His hair sparkles with scattered fish scales. So does mine. Often we spread a picnic: black bread, smelly cheese, a tin of sardines. I eat only my share.

At nineteen, during my college vacation, I fly out to join my parents in Japan. My father and I climb Mount Fuji. High above the Pacific, and hours up the cindery slope, we picnic on dried eel, seaweed crackers, cold rice wrapped in the skin of an eel. He reaches the peak first.

Through years we hike along a beach in Cyprus,[17] beside a river in Lebanon,[18] the Seine,[19]

---

[15]samovar: urn
[16]Tula: Russian city
[17]Cyprus: island south of Turkey
[18]Lebanon: Asian nation
[19]Seine: French river

Alpine[20] streams, and picnic by various other waters and weathers. We overtake one another. I've never known anyone with such energy.

*   *   *

Time rots like old fish.

Today in the nursing home in Virginia I beg him, "*Please*, Daddy, just a little walk. You are supposed to exercise."

The nurses are supposed to walk him daily, but they are always too busy. I try to walk him whenever I visit, but seldom lately has he felt up to more than a step or two.

"Come, Daddy, forward, march . . ."

He can't get out of his chair. I've forgotten to untie the straps of the "posey" which restrains him. Not that he often gets up on his own, but once in a while he'll suddenly have a spurt of strength, then is like to topple over. I crouch to lift his feet from the foot pedals, fold back the metal pieces which too often bruise his paperthin skin.

"Come, now you can stand."

He struggles, but cannot move. I place his hands on the rubberized handholds on the metal walker. "Hold tightly and you can pull yourself up."

He grips the walker and struggles forward. He still cannot make it to his feet. I am about to lift him, when the nurse comes down the corridor.[21]

"Lunch trays are up," she calls out. "Everyone hurry to the solarium!"[22]

As if anyone here could do much hurrying.

I push his wheelchair to the dining room. His plastic plate is heaped with pureed[23] tuna—he's been

---

[20]Alpine: of the Alps, European mountain range
[21]corridor: hall
[22]solarium: room with large windows to admit sunlight
[23]pureed: finely ground

having trouble swallowing lately—but he ignores his lunch. The ice cream turns to milk in its styrofoam dish.

I hand him a spoon. It slips from his fingers. Some days I sing him old songs, tell stories, but one of the residents turns the television on full blast and he can't even hear my repeated, "Won't you eat, Daddy, please?"

I lift a spoonful of grey fishy stuff to his mouth.

He whispers, politely, "I don't care for any."

Nor would I.

Suddenly I go into action, wheel him to the nurses' station, sign him out for the afternoon. It has been a while since I've taken him out, the weather has been too cold or too hot, I haven't had time between work and children and travels, he has had so many bad days of late, he has often been asleep when I've come by, it's a hassle to get him into the car, and how much would he take in any more anyway.

We head fullspeed for the elevator, downstairs, out the main door, out into the parking lot. An orderly[24] helps me get him into my car, and fits the folded wheelchair into the trunk. I adjust our seat belts.

Off we go, down the road, over the bridge toward town.

"We're crossing the Potomac River now, Daddy. Ahead are the Kennedy Center and Watergate, and to the right—can you see the Washington Monument? Remember when we climbed up there, ignored the elevator? And the Smithsonian Museum—how many rainy Saturdays did we spend in museums? And look at those flower beds—"

---

[24] orderly: hospital aide

He doesn't say much to my running travelogue,[25] but seems to be staring out the car window and taking in at least something of a scene he used to know well. The sky is very blue, and so is the river.

We turn south from Independence Avenue past some warehouses and pull in by my favorite wholesale fish market.

"I'll be back in a moment, Daddy. Please wait for me—"

As if he had a choice.

Inside the cool building men in hip boots are sloshing[26] around carrying 16-pound sea trout by the tails. Fish scales fly through the moist air. Frozen boxes of squid and string bags of clams are awaiting pick-up for some restaurant. A curly-haired man is hosing down the floor. I step over the puddles and ask him if by any chance he has any eel today.

"We haven't had any in a year, Ma'am. But it just happens that today—if you don't mind smoked eel—"

He wraps a large chunk in waxy white paper. I pay and hurry out to the car where my father is watching with interest a forklift loading crates of mussels into a truck.

"I've brought you a surprise."

"Why, thank you, dear!" His voice is stronger than I've heard it for months, and he stretches forward for the package with interest. He loves presents, and reaches with awkward fingers to try to open it. The smell fills the car. His fingers can't undo it, but he holds it while I drive down to the river and find a parking place near the marina.[27] Somehow I wrestle

---

[25] travelogue: talk about a trip
[26] sloshing: splashing
[27] marina: dock

the wheelchair from the car, set it up, wrestle him into it, push him out to a level area.

"I'd like a bit of a walk," he says clearly.

Gradually I lift and push and pull him to his feet. Now he is standing, unsteadily, then gains a sort of balance.

"See, you made it! That's wonderful . . . First take a deep breath . . . All right? I'll be right behind you, my hand is in the small of your back. Now—Forward, march!"

He shuffles a couple of steps along the quai.[28] I am holding him securely, somehow maneuvering[29] the wheelchair behind him in case he gets tired. I steady him as he pauses to watch the sail and motor boats on the river. He manages a few more steps, and a few more, along the quai. He hasn't walked this far in months, and seems pleased with himself. There is a small bench ahead and, abandoning the wheelchair, we sit down together.

Again for the first time in months, he begins to talk. He remarks on the red dress of a buxom[30] young woman striding by, he wonders what day it is, he inquires about the children. It is some sort of a miracle, this return to "normalcy," however brief. I cherish every instant.

"And what about your dinner plans?" he asks with his old graciousness, and invites me out for supper. Of course I accept, we'll manage it somehow. Meanwhile, it is only mid-afternoon, too soon for restaurants, but he has worked up an appetite.

---

[28]quai: long wharf or dock
[29]maneuvering: skillfully guiding
[30]buxom: large-breasted

I run over and buy something like lemonade from a vendor.[31] Then I take the small smelly package wrapped in glazed ivory paper from its plastic bag.

"Look, Daddy. The fishmonger[32] actually had some smoked eel."

We unwrap it, then I take out the Swiss Army knife my step-mother gave me "for safekeeping," open the bottles and thinly slice the silvery flesh.

"What a beautiful picnic," my father beams.

He takes a swig[33] of the lemonade, then with steady fingers picks up a slice of eel and downs it without difficulty. Then another, and another, until he eats the whole chunk.

---

[31] vendor: seller
[32] fishmonger: seller of fish
[33] swig: gulp

REFLECT ·

What were some of the problems troubling the mother in "Lost in America"?

In "The Parrot's Beak," what did Kartar Dhillon's mother do to help ensure her daughters' happiness? How did Dhillon react when her mother told her what she had done? Why?

In "Friend or Father?" Anthony Walton's father sums up what he has learned from life in adages—brief statements of advice. What advice does he give his son? What does the advice say about the father as a person?

What made Elisavietta Ritchie ("In Search of Eels") take her father on an outing? What memories did the smoked eel trigger in her mind?

Elisavietta Ritchie uses a lot of specific details in her writing. Find examples of description that appeals to each of the five senses.

Which readings show a parent acting as a traditional authority figure? Which show a child acting like a parent toward his or her parent?

WRITE ·································

Write a note to a parent or guardian thanking the person for his or her help.

In "Friend or Father?" Anthony Walton describes lessons that he learned from his father. Describe a time when you learned a lesson in life from an older person.

The taste of smoked eels brings back happy memories for Elisavietta Ritchie and her father in "In Search of Eels." Describe a food, aroma, piece of music, or other sensory experience that triggers happy memories in your mind. Begin by describing the sensory experience in the present; then flash back to the past, and describe the memory the experience triggers.

Over twenty million of today's Americans came to this country from other lands. They have helped make the United States the first "universal nation"—a country made up of many different cultures and traditions.

CAUGHT BETWEEN CULTURES

What does the word *culture* mean to you? A dictionary will tell you that a culture is all the beliefs and patterns of behavior that set one group of people apart from another. But what would you say if someone asked you to describe the culture you live in? Your culture surrounds you as naturally as the air you breathe—and it can be just as hard to see. Most of us aren't really aware of our culture until we come into contact with a different one.

The readings that follow show people coping with life in two different worlds—their native cultures and mainstream United States culture. The people face many problems—racism, prejudice, learning a new language, adjusting to a new way of life. In each case, they take pride in their roots while finding ways to fit in with United States culture at large.

As you read, put yourself in the place of the people being described. Ask yourself what you would have done in each situation.

Sarah (Sadie) Delany, 104 years old, and her sister Annie Elizabeth (Bessie) Delany, 102, are remarkable women. The Delanys' father was born a slave, yet went on to become the nation's first African-American Episcopal bishop. Both sisters not only were graduated from college but also went on to earn advanced degrees. Bessie became a dentist; Sadie, a teacher.

In the following reading, Sadie describes how she broke new ground as the first black teacher in an all-white high school. As you read, notice the friendly, familiar way she talks to her readers. Think also about the courage it took to do what she did.

Around Brick Walls

From *Having Our Say*
Sarah Delany

I had wanted to teach at a high school because it was considered a promotion, and it paid better. But I had to be a little clever—Bessie would say sneaky—to find ways to get around these brick walls they set up for colored folks. So I asked around quietly for some advice. A friend of my brother Hubert's who worked for the Board of Education suggested a plan, which I followed.

This is what I did: I applied for a high school position, and when I reached the top of the seniority[1]

---

[1] seniority: status earned by number of years on the job

list after three years, I received a letter in the mail saying they wished to meet with me in person. At the appointment, they would have seen I was colored and found some excuse to bounce me down the list. So I skipped the appointment and sent them a letter, acting like there was a mix-up. Then I just showed up on the first day of classes. It was risky, but I knew what a bureaucracy[2] it was, and that in a bureaucracy it's easier to keep people out than to push them back down.

Child, when I showed up that day—at Theodore Roosevelt High School, a white high school—they just about died when they saw me. A colored woman! But my name was on the list to teach there, and it was too late for them to send me someplace else. The plan had worked! Once I was in, they couldn't figure out how to get rid of me.

So I became the first colored teacher in the New York City system to teach domestic science[3] on the high school level. I spent the rest of my career teaching at excellent high schools! Between 1930 and 1960, when I retired, I taught at Theodore Roosevelt High School, which is on Fordham Road in the Bronx, then at Girls' High School in Brooklyn, and finally at Evander Childs High School, which is on Gun Hill Road in the Bronx.

Plus, I got a night job—at Washington Irving High School in lower Manhattan—teaching adults who had dropped out of school. This was something I really wanted to do. The way I got the job was that the girl who had it before me complained a lot, was late a lot, and would ask me to substitute for her. Eventually, they just hired me instead of her! But

---

[2]bureaucracy: complicated system of officials
[3]domestic science: cooking and sewing

that's the way you get ahead, child. Even if you're colored, if you're good enough, you'll get the job. As long as they *need* you, you've got that job.

Meanwhile, I was studying for my master's degree in education at Columbia, which I completed in 1925. I was a busy gal, but I was happy being busy: My classes were usually very demanding because as a colored teacher, I always got the meanest kids. Except once. That was the year they had me mixed up with a white woman whose name also was Delany. It was kind of funny. She was just furious, because she got all these tough girls, and I got the easy ones—college-bound and motivated. Tell you the truth, I did not mind the tough kids. I loved them all.

It was lonely being about the only colored teacher around. Sometimes the white teachers were friendly, but you couldn't count on any of them being your real friends. There was one woman I was friendly with, and we decided to meet on a Saturday and go swimming at a public pool in the Bronx. I remember that when she saw me in my bathing suit, she looked at my legs and said, "Why, Sarah, you are very white!" And I said, "So what?" I guess she was surprised that I didn't try to pass for[4] white.

Personally, I never had any desire to be white. I am absolutely comfortable with who I am. I used to laugh at how both races seem to hate their hair. All these Negro ladies would run out and get their hair *straightened*, and all these white ladies would run out and get their hair *curled*. My hair was in-between, with a little kink in it, just enough to give it body. I had no desire to change it. I had no desire to change me. I guess I owe that to my Mama and Papa.

---

[4]pass for: pretend to be

This same teacher who seemed to wonder why I didn't just try to "pass" turned out to be a fair-weather friend. Once, she and I had planned to go swimming, and she said to wait under the clock at noon, and so I did. But coincidentally, some other white girls she knew showed up right when she arrived. So she just snubbed me. She didn't want them to know we were friends, so she left me standing there and walked on past, with them. She was so obvious that there really wasn't anything to do but laugh it off and forget about it.

I remained on friendly terms with that woman. Bessie says, "I wouldn't have had nothing more to do with her this side of Glory!" This is the kind of thing that drives Bessie wild. Bessie would have given her a piece of her mind. Sure, it annoyed me. But I didn't let it ruin my day. Life is short, and it's up to you to make it sweet.

*Andrea Martínez is a Zapotec Indian.
The Zapotecs are native to Mexico but
have their own language and customs.
As a teenager, Martínez and her family
moved to the United States. Even though
they moved to a largely Mexican-American community in California, Martínez
felt very alone. As a stranger to both
Mexican and United States cultures, she
had to make two adjustments at once.*

Fitting In

In *Voices from the Fields*
S. Beth Atkin

I am from El Mirado, a village near the town of Oji-
tlan, by the city of Tuxtepect, in the state of Oaxaca,
Mexico. I am a Zapotec *indio.*[1] Zapotec is a kind of
indigena[2] group from Mexico. The dialect we speak
is Zapoteca. My grandparents are Zapotec and were
born on the *ranchita*[3] I lived on, and they worked off
the land, planting seeds, harvesting the crops, and
selling them if there was extra. My mother grew up
there also. My real father was from around there, too.
But I never really knew him. My grandmother raised
me so my mother could work in Mexico City.

I started working on the *ranchita* when I was
eight, harvesting chilies, corn, and coffee. Lots of
children did the same. There were about fifty families
living in our community then. Everyone had their

---

[1] *indio*: Indian
[2] *indigena*: native
[3] *ranchita*: small ranch

own land, which had been divided up by a committee. The committee was also supposed to collect money for the school. But most of the parents said the school didn't work. They preferred their children to work in the fields instead of studying. Many people where I grew up thought that if you are a girl, you are just supposed to get married. That is what my grandmother thought, so I worked, and my brothers went to school. My grandmother told me, "Since you are a girl, you are not supposed to study." She thought that girls were lowly. So as you can see, I have known discrimination[4] since I was small. Another way I've known it is growing up in Mexico and being Zapotec. Even though we come from the same blood, the Mexicans would discriminate against us because we were Indian. They would say, "Indio, get to work." That is because we are poor, and we had to work hard.

I moved to the Salinas Valley[5] four years ago with my mother and my brother Francisco. My brother Sergio stayed in Mexico. I have a little sister, also, named Marilyn. She was born here just a year ago. My stepfather, who is her father, came with us from Mexico, too, but I didn't know him because my mother met him when she left the *ranchita*. My mother first worked here mostly in the grapes. But now I don't get to see her much because she works a lot in Yuma, Arizona, in *la lechuga*.[6] It's difficult, and every day I miss her. When we first moved I felt alone here. My mother would leave to work, and it was really hard because my stepfather only speaks Spanish. I couldn't talk to him because I only spoke Zapoteca. Where I

---

[4] discrimination: prejudice
[5] Salinas Valley: area of California known for its farmlands
[6] *la lechuga*: the lettuce

grew up, the only time I ever heard Spanish was when an outsider came and someone would talk in Spanish out of need. If someone spoke to us in Spanish, we were afraid because we didn't understand what they were saying. We were also embarrassed that we couldn't talk back to them.

Everything here was different from where I grew up: the food, the people, the clothes. But the hardest part for me when I moved was the language. I couldn't speak Spanish, and I didn't know English. Also no one in my community in Mexico knew how to write or even how to pick up a pencil. My mother told me that things would be better soon because here at least I could get an education.

There is nothing similar about Zapoteca and Spanish, and it took me a year just to learn Spanish. My stepfather talked to one of my teachers and explained that I didn't know Spanish. In my Spanish class the teacher had her aide help me a lot. Little by little, she taught me how to make sentences. But learning English was harder. I stayed in the same level for two years. The English class had all Mexicans, and I had a classmate who tried to help me a lot. She is still my friend. But she only spoke Spanish, and so I didn't really understand. In other subjects, I was put in classes that were too advanced for me because I didn't know the language. Like in social studies: the teacher told me I should raise my hand more in class. She knew that I had the answers, like the capitals of countries in Central America. But I didn't know how to say the answers. So I stayed after school, and she helped me. Then I advanced in the class and got an A. I was lucky because a lot of teachers helped me.

My mother encouraged me a lot when she was home. I didn't know how to defend myself, and she helped me. She told me to try to speak in Spanish and not to quit even though the students were making fun of me. They pulled my hair and they called me a *mensa*.[7] They insulted me. The *pochas* especially—their parents are from Mexico but they were born here and speak mostly English. They think they are great and that once they know a little English they are *gabachas*.[8] They called me "*indio*" to insult me because that is what they call people who just came from Mexico. But what they didn't know is that I am a true Indian.

For me, the *pochas* are worse than the *gabachas*. The time I went on a field trip, for the FBLA (Future Business Leaders of America), everybody treated me well. They weren't Mexican, and when I told them I couldn't speak English well, they said, "Andrea, you can speak very well." I've also taken an English literature class, and no one American made fun of me. But I know that some Mexicans here have problems and are treated badly. In King City, which is right nearby, some high school students want a school newspaper in Spanish, but the school won't let them have it. So maybe it is easier here for Americans than Mexicans. But I'm not sure because I usually don't see what problems Americans confront, only the ones Mexicans have. What I do think is Americans educate their children better.

The hardest problem for Mexicans is that they need to know English to live here. They have a hard time knowing only Spanish. But most of them have had an education in Mexico. There are not a lot of students who have had to face what I did. It's not that I'm the only one, but when I moved to the United States, I hadn't gone to school, and I couldn't communicate at all.

---

[7] *mensa*: fool
[8] *gabachas*: non-Mexicans

Now things are better because I have friends. Before if some girls would walk by me and say, "Hi. How are you?" I was too embarrassed to talk to them in Spanish. I was afraid. Now I'm not. Also, since I've come here I have had the opportunity for an education and I'm learning a lot. One of the best experiences we had is going to the Yo Puedo [I Can] program. It is a special summer program at a college campus in Santa Cruz that helps children of migrant workers. It motivates them to go forward and improve their lives. A lot of people helped me with the Yo Puedo application, and I got in. Just getting accepted gave me more confidence because I never thought I would. Nobody made fun of me there, and being at a university was really nice. The program helped me in many ways. I learned computers there, and now I want to become a computer engineer when I go to college. It also made me more comfortable to be in the United States.

Now that I have finished the program, I'm still learning through Advanced Leadership Training sessions. Once a month, all the Yo Puedo students teach little migrant children to try hard and be motivated in school. I tell them to never quit school. We have workshops and do skits on subjects like self-esteem, language barriers, and discrimination. One day I will stand up and speak at a workshop on discrimination. Because the kids in the program should see that it's not just the Americans that discriminate against us but also Mexicans who are born here, the *pochas*, who discriminate against other Mexicans, too. I don't want to offend them but I would tell them, "You will know what it is like when you go to university and feel discrimination, because Americans will see you as Mexican." Then maybe they will notice that discrimination is everywhere.

Since I have been here for a while, I now know what it feels like to be Mexican. I speak Spanish and have friends that are Mexican. But I still think my Zapotec heritage is important. I don't speak my dialect much, because my mother isn't around. But I try to think about it by myself. It is important not to lose it, because it is in my blood. If I had to choose between being Mexican and Zapotec, I'd choose both. Because I can't discriminate against Zapotecas, my people.

Adam Hryniewicki moved to the United States from Poland in the late 1980s. Like many newcomers, Hryniewicki likes life in the United States but finds some American customs hard to get used to.

Interview with Adam Hryniewicki

From *Home of the Brave*
Mary Motley Kalergis

I came here a couple of years ago. I always wanted to come to America. My mother told me that if I want to leave Poland, Germany is for Germans and France is for the French, but the United States is for everyone. From my graduating class of thirty in Danzig, there are only about ten people left in the country. All the ambitious young people have to leave if they want to achieve their goals. It's a shame for my country, but you can't control people and keep them satisfied. I came to America with a round-trip ticket, but I knew I would want to stay here. There was no way I could stay in Poland. The only way to have a nice life there is to be a bad person—totally corrupt.[1] Here in America I can make a nice life for myself and mind my own business.

Even though I knew no English, I found a Polish man who gave me a job after I'd been here for about six weeks. I worked sometimes ten to twelve hours a day for not much pay. All I did was work and sleep. Later I met another man who would pay me by the hour, which seemed a lot more fair. Being an electri-

---

[1] corrupt: unethical; without regard for right and wrong

cian, it's pretty easy for me to find work. I'm lucky to have a skill that translates into English. It's very hard to get a license in New Jersey, but I work as a subcontractor for a licensed electrician. I get paid pretty well. I'm beginning to do painting and carpeting and carpentry as well.

I feel a lot less frustrated living here. I feel like I have more control over my future. Good ideas are valued here. A lot of people get rich off a clever idea. The key to success here is to maintain your focus. You lose your focus and you lose yourself. Anything you want is here, if you know what you want. The little things like the food you eat and the clothes you wear—there are so many choices. One thing I really like about this country is knowing people from different backgrounds. I don't want to live only in a Polish community. I want to assimilate,[2] but I was born and educated in Poland and will always be a Polish-American. I can make a lot of money here in a very short time, but the quality of life in the Northeast is not so nice. After I've saved up some money, I'd like to travel to other parts of the country and maybe settle in the South or the West.

One American habit I don't understand is buying on credit. I don't believe in working so hard just to pay off the interest and you still have your debt. America is a factory of interest. I never buy anything unless I can pay for it. I don't want to owe anyone anything because then I wouldn't be a free man. It's unbelievable to me that American parents charge their grown children rent to live at home. I don't understand this attitude toward money. If you care about money too much, it's hard to be a kind person.

---

[2]assimilate: be absorbed into the mainstream culture

Lewis Sawaquat is a Potawatomi Ottawa Indian. In this reading, Sawaquat explains how he was an adult before he truly accepted or even knew much about his roots. He talks about the misunderstandings and prejudices he has faced as a Native American and what his daughter will face as she grows up in both cultures.

For My Indian Daughter

In *Newsweek*
Lewis Sawaquat

My little girl is singing herself to sleep upstairs, her voice mingling with the sounds of the birds outside in the old maple trees. She is two and I am nearly 50, and I am very taken with her. She came along late in my life, unexpected and unbidden,[1] a startling[2] gift.

Today at the beach my chubby-legged, brown-skinned daughter ran laughing into the water as fast as she could. My wife and I laughed watching her, until we heard behind us a low guttural[3] curse and then an unpleasant voice raised in an imitation war whoop.

I turned to see a fat man in a bathing suit, white and soft as a grub,[4] as he covered his mouth and prepared to make the Indian war cry again. He was middle-aged, younger than I, and had three little chil-

---

[1] unbidden: not asked for
[2] startling: surprising
[3] guttural: low-pitched; growling
[4] grub: worm

dren lined up next to him, grinning foolishly. My wife suggested we leave the beach, and I agreed.

I knew the man was not unusual in his feelings against Indians. His beach behavior might have been socially unacceptable[5] to more civilized whites, but his basic view of Indians is expressed daily in our small town, frequently[6] on the editorial pages of the county newspaper, as white people speak out against Indian fishing rights and land rights, saying in essence,[7] "Those Indians are taking our fish, our land." It doesn't matter to them that we were here first, that the U.S. Supreme Court has ruled in our favor. It matters to them that we have something they want, and they hate us for it. Backlash[8] is the common explanation of the attacks on Indians, the bumper stickers that say, "Spear an Indian, Save a Fish," but I know better. The hatred of Indians goes back to the beginning when white people came to this country. For me it goes back to my childhood in Harbor Springs, Michigan.

Theft

Harbor Springs is now a summer resort for the very affluent,[9] but a hundred years ago it was the Indian Village of my Ottawa ancestors. My grandmother, Anna Showanessy, and other Indians like her, had their land there taken by treaty, by fraud,[10] by violence, by theft. They remembered how whites had

---

[5] socially unacceptable: frowned upon
[6] frequently: often
[7] in essence: in a nutshell
[8] backlash: strongly negative reaction
[9] affluent: rich
[10] fraud: cheating

burned down the village at Burt Lake in 1900 and pushed the Indians out. These were the stories in my family.

When I was a boy my mother told me to walk down the alleys in Harbor Springs and not to wear my orange football sweater out of the house. This way I would not stand out, not be noticed, and not be a target.

I wore my orange sweater anyway and deliberately[11] avoided the alleys. I was the biggest person I knew and wasn't really afraid. But I met my comeuppance[12] when I enlisted in the U.S. Army. One night all the men in my barracks[13] gathered together and, gang-fashion, pulled me into the shower and scrubbed me down with rough brushes used for floors, saying "We won't have any dirty Indians in our outfit." It is a point of irony[14] that I was cleaner than any of them. Later in Korea I learned how to kill, how to bully, how to hate Koreans. I came out of the war tougher than ever and, strangely, white.

I went to college, got married, lived in La Porte, Indiana, worked as a surveyor[15] and raised three boys. I headed Boy Scout groups, never thinking it odd when the Scouts did imitation Indian dances, imitation Indian lore.[16]

---

[11]deliberately: on purpose

[12]comeuppance: just deserts; punishment

[13]barracks: military housing

[14]point of irony: truth that is the opposite of what one might expect

[15]surveyor: one who measures plots of land

[16]lore: tradition

One day when I was 35 or thereabouts I heard about an Indian powwow.[17] My father used to attend them and so with great curiosity and a strange joy at discovering a part of my heritage,[18] I decided the thing to do to get ready for this big event was to have my friend make me a spear in his forge.[19] The steel was fine and blue and iridescent.[20] The feathers on the shaft were bright and proud.

In a dusty state fairground in southern Indiana, I found white people dressed as Indians. I learned they were "hobbyists," that is, it was their hobby and leisure pastime to masquerade[21] as Indians on weekends. I felt ridiculous with my spear, and I left.

It was years before I could tell anyone of the embarrassment of this weekend and see any humor in it. But in a way it was that weekend, for all its silliness, that was my awakening. I realized I didn't know who I was. I didn't have an Indian name. I didn't speak the Indian language. I didn't know the Indian customs. Dimly I remembered the Ottawa word for dog, but it was a baby word, *kahgee*, not the full word, *muhkahgee*, which I was later to learn. Even more hazily I remembered a naming ceremony (my own). I remember legs dancing around me, dust. Where had that been? Who had I been? "Suwaukquat," my mother told me when I asked, "where the tree begins to grow."

---

[17]powwow: Indian ceremony
[18]heritage: roots
[19]forge: metal shop
[20]iridescent: brightly colored as in a rainbow
[21]masquerade: dress up

That was 1968, and I was not the only Indian in the country who was feeling the need to remember who he or she was. There were others. They had powwows, real ones, and eventually I found them. Together we researched our past, a search that for me culminated[22] in the Longest Walk, a march on Washington in 1978. Maybe because I now know what it means to be Indian, it surprises me that others don't. Of course there aren't very many of us left. The chances of an average person knowing an average Indian in an average lifetime are pretty slim.

Circle

Still, I was amused one day when my small, four-year-old neighbor looked at me as I was hoeing in my garden and said, "You aren't a real Indian, are you?" Scotty is little, talkative, likable. Finally I said, "I'm a real Indian." He looked at me for a moment and then said, squinting into the sun, "Then where's your horse and feathers?" The child was simply a smaller, whiter version of my own ignorant self years before. We'd both seen too much TV, that's all. He was not to be blamed. And so, in a way, the moronic[23] man on the beach today is blameless. We come full circle to realize other people are like ourselves, as discomfiting[24] as that may be sometimes.

As I sit in my old chair on my porch, in a light that is fading so the leaves are barely distinguishable[25] against the sky, I can picture my girl

---

[22]culminated: reached a high point
[23]moronic: stupid
[24]discomfiting: unsettling
[25]distinguishable: able to be seen

asleep upstairs. I would like to prepare her for what's to come, take her each step of the way saying, there's a place to avoid, here's what I know about this, but much of what's before her she must go through alone. She must pass through pain and joy and solitude[26] and community to discover her own inner self that is unlike any other and come through that passage to the place where she sees all people are one, and in so seeing may live her life in a brighter future.

---

[26] solitude: aloneness

REFLECT ··································

How did Sarah Delany ("Around Brick Walls") trick the local board of education into hiring her?

How does Delany feel about her African-American roots? The prejudice that has been directed at her?

What difficulties has Andrea Martínez ("Fitting In") had to overcome?

What does Adam Hryniewicki ("Interview . . .") like about life in the United States? Dislike?

Some people still view Native Americans as stereotypes rather than as individuals. In your opinion, what causes people to stereotype others? What effects have negative stereotypes of Native Americans had on Lewis Sawaquat ("For My Indian Daughter")?

Sawaquat calls the second part of his article "Theft." What was stolen from him? Why does he give the name "Circle" to the last part of the article?

Sarah Delany says, "Life is short, and it's up to you to make it sweet." How do you think Andrea Martínez, Adam Hryniewicki, and Lewis Sawaquat would respond to this statement?

WRITE ·

Adam Hryniewicki mentions things that he likes and
dislikes about life in the United States. Which
aspects of life in the United States do you especially
appreciate? Which would you most like to change?

Write about an incidence of prejudice that you saw or
were a part of. What happened? How did you feel? If
you could relive the situation, would you react the
same way?

Put yourself in the place of Lewis Sawaquat. Would
you want your daughter to identify herself as a Native
American? Or would you avoid teaching her about
her roots to help her more easily fit in with the
mainstream? Explain.

A grandmother and granddaughter enjoy each other's company. They show their love by making time for each other.

ACTS OF KINDNESS AND LOVE

Think about the best gift you've ever given or received—not the most expensive, but the one that counted the most. What was the gift? What made it so special? Wasn't it that it showed how much you cared about someone or how much someone cared about you?

Gifts are only one of the ways we show we care. Small acts of kindness—thoughtful things we do for one another—are also expressions of love.

The four readings that follow are about acts of kindness and love. The ways this kindness and love are shown are as different as the people involved.

As you read, think about the people in each of the readings. Imagine what motivated them to be so unselfish—and what results their acts of kindness and love produced.

Bob Greene is an award-winning writer whose column appears in newspapers across the country.

The death of someone we love is a painful experience. It is even more painful when we don't have a chance to say a last good-bye. In this reading, Greene tells the story of a little girl's love for her grandfather and the unusual way that love was returned.

Above and Beyond

In *He Was a Midwestern Boy on His Own*
Bob Greene

When Bernie Meyers, who was seventy years old and who lived in Wilmette, Illinois, went into the hospital last September, his family at first did not know how serious his illness was. Thus his ten-year-old granddaughter, Sarah Meyers, was not taken to see him.

"He hadn't been feeling well for some time," said Sarah's mother, Ann Meyers. "He went into the hospital for some tests. Just to find out what was wrong."

What was wrong was lymphoma—a cancer of the lymphatic system. In Bernie Meyers' case, the lymphoma was advanced and irreversible.[1] He died within two weeks.

Sarah Meyers never got a chance to say good-bye to her grandfather.

"Sarah saw him regularly, because we live close to where he lived," her mother said. "This was her

---
[1] irreversible: incurable

first experience with death. We could tell that, as upset as she was, she was additionally upset that she didn't see him in those days before he died. She didn't get to have one last talk with him."

Sarah didn't say much about what she was feeling. But in October she came home from a friend's birthday party. The other children at the party had been given helium balloons as favors. Sarah had hers with her—a bright red balloon.

"She went into the house," her mother said. "When she came back out, she was carrying the balloon—and an envelope."

Inside the envelope was a letter she had written to her grandfather. The envelope was addressed to "Grandpa Bernie, in Heaven Up High." In the letter, Sarah wrote: "Hi, Grandpa. How are you? What's it like up there?" The letter ended with Sarah telling her grandfather that she loved him, and that she hoped somehow he could hear what she was telling him.

"I'm not sure what Sarah's concept of heaven is," her mother said. "But I do know that she printed our return address on the envelope. I didn't ask her about it. She punched a hole in the envelope, and tied the envelope to the balloon. Then she let it go.

"That balloon seemed so fragile[2] to me. I didn't think it would even make it past the trees. But it did. We watched the balloon sail away, and then we went back inside."

Two months passed; the weather got cold. Then one day a letter arrived addressed to "Sarah Meyers + Family." The letter bore a York, Pennsylvania, postmark, and had been mailed by a man named Donald H. Kopp.

---

[2] fragile: easily broken

The letter began:

> Dear Sarah, Family & Friends—
> Your letter to Grandpa Bernie Meyers apparently reached its destination and was read by him. I understand they can't keep material things up there, so it drifted back to earth. They just keep thoughts, memories, love, and things like that.

Donald Kopp wrote that he had found the balloon and letter while hunting and hiking in a Pennsylvania state forest near the Maryland border. That is almost six hundred miles from Wilmette—the balloon had floated over Illinois, probably parts of Michigan and Indiana, Ohio, and all the way across Pennsylvania before settling in the forest.

Donald Kopp's letter to Sarah continued:

> Whenever you think or talk about your grandpa, he knows and is very close by with overwhelming love. Sincerely, Don Kopp. (Also a grandpa.)

Sarah said that after she had tied her letter to the balloon and let it float away, "At night I would think about it. I just wanted to hear from Grandpa somehow. In a way, now I think that I have heard from him."

Donald Kopp, who is sixty-three and retired from his job as a receiving clerk, said the other day that the red balloon, which had almost completely deflated, was resting on a blueberry bush the afternoon he found it.

"That's pretty dense woods," he said. "It was cold and windy that day. I walked over to see what the balloon was. I could tell it was a child's handwriting on the envelope. I didn't have my reading glasses on, and I thought it was addressed to someone at 'Haven High.' A high school or something.

"I put it in my pocket. When I got back home, I saw that it wasn't addressed to Haven High. It was addressed to Sarah's grandfather, in 'Heaven Up High.' "

So he decided to write his letter to Sarah. "It was important to me that I write to her," he said. "But I'm not very good at writing; I don't do it that often. It took me a couple of days to think of what to put in the letter. Then I mailed it.

"Like I said in the letter—I'm a grandfather, too."

Robert Fulghum has been a cowboy, a computer salesman, an artist, a singer, a Unitarian minister, a bartender, and, of course, a writer. His first book, All I Really Need to Know I Learned in Kindergarten, *was a bestseller. In the following reading, Fulghum describes how he was once given a wonderful gift but didn't immediately recognize its value.*

The Good Stuff

In *It Was on Fire When I Lay Down on It*
Robert Fulghum

The cardboard box is marked "The Good Stuff." As I write, I can see the box where it is stored on a high shelf in my studio.[1] I like being able to see it when I look up. The box contains those odds and ends of personal treasures that have survived many bouts[2] of clean-it-out-and-throw-it-away that seize me from time to time. The box has passed through the screening done as I've moved from house to house and hauled stuff from attic to attic. A thief looking into the box would not take anything—he couldn't get a dime for any of it. But if the house ever catches on fire, the box goes with me when I run.

One of the keepsakes[3] in the box is a small paper bag. Lunch size. Though the top is sealed with duct tape, staples, and several paper clips, there is a ragged rip in one side through which the contents may be seen.

---

[1] studio: place where a writer, artist, or other craftsperson creates
[2] bouts: rounds
[3] keepsakes: souvenirs

This particular lunch sack has been in my care for maybe fourteen years. But it really belongs to my daughter, Molly. Soon after she came of school age, she became an enthusiastic participant in packing the morning lunches for herself, her brothers, and me. Each bag got a share of sandwiches, apples, milk money, and sometimes a note or a treat. One morning Molly handed me two bags as I was about to leave. One regular sack. And the one with the duct tape and staples and paper clips. "Why two bags?" "The other one is something else." "What's in it?" "Just some stuff—take it with you." Not wanting to hold court over[4] the matter, I stuffed both sacks into my briefcase, kissed the child, and rushed off.

At midday, while hurriedly scarfing[5] down my real lunch, I tore open Molly's bag and shook out the contents. Two hair ribbons, three small stones, a plastic dinosaur, a pencil stub, a tiny seashell, two animal crackers, a marble, a used lipstick, a small doll, two chocolate kisses, and thirteen pennies.

I smiled. How charming. Rising to hustle off to all the important business of the afternoon, I swept the desk clean—into the wastebasket—leftover lunch, Molly's junk, and all. There wasn't anything in there I needed.

That evening Molly came to stand beside me while I was reading the paper. "Where's my bag?" "What bag?" "You know, the one I gave you this morning." "I left it at the office, why?" "I forgot to put this note in it." She hands over the note. "Besides, I want it back?" "Why?" "Those are my things in the sack, Daddy, the ones I really like—I thought you might like to play with them, but now I

---

[4] hold court over: spend time questioning
[5] scarfing: gobbling

want them back. You didn't lose the bag, did you, Daddy?" Tears puddled in her eyes. "Oh no, I just forgot to bring it home," I lied. "Bring it tomorrow, okay?" "Sure thing—don't worry." As she hugged my neck with relief, I unfolded the note that had not got into the sack: "I love you, Daddy."

Oh.

And also—uh-oh.

I looked long at the face of my child.

She was right—what was in that sack was "something else."

Molly had given me her treasures. All that a seven-year-old held dear. Love in a paper sack. And I had missed it. Not only missed it, but had thrown it in the wastebasket because "there wasn't anything in there I needed." Dear God.

It wasn't the first or the last time I felt my Daddy Permit[6] was about to run out.

It was a long trip back to the office. But there was nothing else to be done. So I went. The pilgrimage of a penitent.[7] Just ahead of the janitor, I picked up the wastebasket and poured the contents on my desk. I was sorting it all out when the janitor came in to do his chores. "Lose something?" "Yeah, my mind." "It's probably in there, all right. What's it look like and I'll help you find it?" I started not to tell him. But I couldn't feel any more of a fool than I was already in fact, so I told him. He didn't laugh. He smiled. "I got kids, too." So the brotherhood of fools searched the trash and found the jewels and he smiled at me and I smiled at him. You are never alone in these things. Never.

---

[6]Daddy Permit: license to be a father
[7]pilgrimage of a penitent: religious journey of one who repents his or her sins

After washing the mustard off the dinosaurs and spraying the whole thing with breath-freshener to kill the smell of onions, I carefully smoothed out the wadded ball of brown paper into a semifunctional[8] bag and put the treasures inside and carried the whole thing home gingerly,[9] like an injured kitten. The next evening I returned it to Molly, no questions asked, no explanations offered. The bag didn't look so good, but the stuff was all there and that's what counted. After dinner I asked her to tell me about the stuff in the sack, and so she took it all out a piece at a time and placed the objects in a row on the dining room table.

It took a long time to tell. Everything had a story, a memory, or was attached to dreams and imaginary friends. Fairies had brought some of the things. And I had given her the chocolate kisses, and she had kept them for when she needed them. I managed to say, "I see" very wisely several times in the telling. And as a matter of fact, I did see.

To my surprise, Molly gave the bag to me once again several days later. Same ratty bag. Same stuff inside. I felt forgiven. And trusted. And loved. And a little more comfortable wearing the title of Father. Over several months the bag went with me from time to time. It was never clear to me why I did or did not get it on a given day. I began to think of it as the Daddy Prize and tried to be good the night before so I might be given it the next morning.

In time Molly turned her attention to other things . . . found other treasures . . . lost interest in the game . . . grew up. Something. Me? I was left holding the

---

8 semifunctional: partly useful
9 gingerly: very carefully

bag. She gave it to me one morning and never asked for its return. And so I have it still.

Sometimes I think of all the times in this sweet life when I must have missed the affection I was being given. A friend calls this "standing knee-deep in the river and dying of thirst."

So the worn paper sack is there in the box. Left over from a time when a child said, "Here—this is the best I've got. Take it—it's yours. Such as I have, give I to thee."

I missed it the first time. But it's my bag now.

Writer Tom Bodett lives in a cabin on the edge of the Alaskan wilderness. His funny radio pieces are a regular part of "All Things Considered," an evening news program on National Public Radio. In the following reading, Bodett uses a story about his grandmother to make a point about the true meaning of charity.

Grandma Hattie

In *As Far As You Can Go Without a Passport*
Tom Bodett

Going through the Christmas cards in our mailbox today, I came across one from my dear old grandma in Illinois. She never fails. Never missed a birthday, Christmas, or anniversary as long as I've lived. Quite a gal, old Grandma Hattie. There's always a nice little letter inside wrapped around a crisp five-dollar bill she can't afford to send.

I read the letter—newsy stuff about her holiday baking and the weather (no snow there yet either). Then as always, there was the postscript at the end: "Just a little Christmas treat. Love, Grandma." So I tucked the five-dollar bill into my shirt and promised that my wife and I would do something extra-special with it. At least as special as five bucks will buy you these days.

Then, as I was reading through the rest of the mail, I came across another card from Grandma. I'll be darned. Must be our anniversary card, being as we were married the day after Christmas, same as her birthday. She never forgets. I was wrong. It was another Christmas card with another newsy little letter and another brand-new five-dollar bill she couldn't afford to send. Well, what do you think of that?

She must have got confused somehow and forgot to cross us off her list. Or maybe she doesn't have a list. She may do it from memory, and eighty-seven-year-old memories can play tricks like that at times. She may have thought she already sent us one but wasn't altogether sure, so she sent another one just in case. That would be just like her. Rather than take the chance of missing one of us by mistake, she'd send two just to be sure. There aren't many of us that can afford the five dollars that would do that. The heck of it is that I don't dare send it back. She'd be so embarrassed by the mistake, it would do her no good, and I'm sure we can get it back to her in other ways.

There's probably not a whole lot of Christmases left in Grandma Hat, and the world will be the worse for it when she goes. She's endeared herself to[1] friends, family, and strangers alike for many, many decades. My mom tells a story of her from the Depression years.

At the time, Grandma and Grandpa owned a dairy. It was right next door to the house, where the garden is now, and they ran it themselves. They lived near the train tracks, and being that it was during the Depression, they used to get their share of hoboes[2] coming around looking for handouts.

They were hard-working folks, my mom's family, and believed that everybody else should be too. They'd give the "bums," as she called them, food and milk, all right. But they'd have to wash milk cans,

---

[1] endeared herself to: beloved by
[2] hoboes: old-fashioned term for homeless people who travel from place to place

scrub floors, shovel snow, or some such thing to get it. Those were the rules, and nobody complained.

Mom says they got pretty popular on the hobo circuit and got that inevitable mark on their front gatepost. Just a little X on the post in white chalk to let the other hoboes know this was a place where a guy could get a handout. It was common practice at that time and was supposed to be on the sly.³ But Grandma knew it was there. She never did bother any with that chalk on the gatepost, except just once.

It was Christmastime, and my mom was just a little girl. They didn't have any snow yet, but right before Christmas they had a big wind and rain storm. Coming back from church that Sunday, Grandma noticed that the chalk mark had been washed clear off the post by the storm.

It got cold right away like it will on the midwestern plains, and snowed to beat the band.⁴ She sat that day in the front room saying the rosary with Grandpa like they always did on Sunday. They saw the hoboes walking down from the train yard going wherever it is hoboes go in a snowstorm. They looked so cold and defeated, but none of them was stopping at the gate or knocking on the dairy window like they always did. Then it struck her why. Of course—the little white X wasn't on the post anymore. Now, where another person might have been relieved to be left alone the Sunday before Christmas, Old Grandma Hat, and she wasn't that old then, put on her overcoat, went right out to the gatepost, and put a great big white X there where nobody could miss it.

---

³on the sly: secret
⁴to beat the band: very heavily

I don't know if they got to feed any hoboes that day or not because Mom usually stops telling the story about there, but it doesn't matter. It told me something abut Grandma, and I've carried this story with me a long time. She put that X on the gatepost way back then for the same reason she sent us two Christmas cards this year. She didn't want to miss anybody, even if it did cost an extra five bucks. I always think of that story when I'm starting to feel a little broke and put out at Christmas; then I'm ashamed of myself.

So I don't know what all this means except that in this hard-hearted world we live in, we should all have a gatepost out front, and at least for this one time of year let's all go out and put a great big white X on that thing.

At one time or another, every one of us has wanted to surprise someone we love with a gift only we could give. In the following reading, a father and son are not able to deliver exactly the gift they planned—yet the love behind the gift brings the family closer together.

The Overspill

In *I Am One of You Forever*
Fred Chappell

There was one brief time when we didn't live in the big brick house with my grandmother but in a neat two-storey green-shingled white house in the holler[1] below. It was two storeys if you stood at the front door; on the other side it was three storeys, the ground floor a tall basement.

The house was surrounded by hills to the north and east and south. Directly above us lay the family farm and my grandmother's house. Two miles behind the south hill was the town of Tipton, where the Challenger Paper and Fiber Corporation smoked eternally, smudging the Carolina mountain landscape for miles. A small creek ran through our side yard, out of the eastern hills. The volume of the creek flow was controlled by Challenger; they had placed a reservoir[2] up there, and the creek water was regulated by means of the spillway.[3]

At this time my mother was visiting her brother in California. Uncle Luden was in trouble again, with

[1] holler: slang for "hollow," a small valley
[2] reservoir: man-made lake where water is stored
[3] spillway: chute that can be opened to release water

a whole different woman this time. Maybe my mother could help; it was only 5,000 miles round trip by train.

So my father and I had to fumble along as best we could.

Despite the extra chores, I found it exciting. Our friendship took a new and stronger turn, became something of a mild conspiracy.[4] New sets of signals evolved[5] between us. We met now on freshly neutral ground somewhere between my boyhood and his boyishness, and for me it was a heady[6] rise in status. We were clumsy housekeepers, there were lots of minor mishaps, and the tagline[7] we formulated soonest was: "Let's just not tell Mom about this one." I adored that thought.

He was always dreaming up new projects to please her and during her absence came up with one of masterful[8] ambition.

Across the little creek, with its rows of tall willows, was a half-acre of fallow[9] ground considered unusable because of marshiness[10] and the impenetrable clot[11] of blackberry vines in the south corner. My father now planned it as a garden, already planted before she returned.

We struggled heroically. I remember pleasantly the destruction of the vines and the cutting of the drainage ditch neat and straight into the field. The ground was so soft that we could slice down with our

---

[4]conspiracy: secret agreement to act together
[5]evolved: developed over time
[6]heady: exciting
[7]tagline: slogan
[8]masterful: powerful
[9]fallow: unused
[10]marshiness: swampiness
[11]impenetrable clot: thick knot

spades[12] and bring up squares of dark blue mud and lay them along side by side. They gleamed like tile. Three long afternoons completed the ditch, and then my father brought out the big awkward shoulder scythe[13] and whetted[14] the blade until I could hear it sing on his thumb-ball when he tested it. And then he waded into the thicket of thorny vine and began slashing. For a long time nothing happened, but finally the vines began to fall back, rolling up in tangles like barbarous[15] handwriting. With a pitchfork I worried[16] these tangles into a heap. Best of all was the firing, the clear yellow flame and the sizzle and snap of the vine-ribs and thorns, and the thin black smoke rising above the new-green willows. The delicious smell of it.

After this we prepared the ground in the usual way and planted. Then we stood at the edge of our garden, admiring with a full tired pride the clean furrows[17] and mounded rows of earth.

But this was only a part of the project. It was merely a vegetable garden, however arduously[18] achieved, and we planted a garden every year. My father wanted something else, decorative, elegant in design, something guaranteed to please a lady.

The weather held good and we started the next day, hauling two loads of scrap lumber from one of the barns. He measured and we sawed and planed. He hummed and whistled as he worked and I mostly

---

[12]spades: shovels
[13]scythe: curved blade used to cut grass and other vegetation
[14]whetted: sharpened
[15]barbarous: wild; uncivilized
[16]worried: tugged repeatedly
[17]furrows: grooves
[18]arduously: with great difficulty

stared at him when not scurrying to and fro, fetching and carrying. He wouldn't, of course, tell me what we were building.

On the second day it became clear. We were constructing a bridge. We were building a small but elaborate[19] bridge across the little creek that divided the yard and the garden, a stream even I could step over without lengthening my stride. It was ambitious: an arched bridge with handrails and a latticework[20] arch on the garden side enclosing a little picket gate.

He must have been a handy carpenter. To me the completed bridge appeared marvelous. We had dug deep on both sides to sink the locust piers,[21] and the arch above the stream, though not high, was unmistakably a rainbow. When I walked back and forth across the bridge I heard and felt a satisfactory drumming. The gate latch made a solid cluck[22] and the gate arch, pinned together of old plaster lathe,[23] made me feel that in crossing the bridge I was entering a different world, not simply going into the garden.

He had further plans for the latticework. "Right here," he said, "and over here, I'll plant tea roses to climb up the lattice. Then you'll see."

We whitewashed it three times. The raw lumber sparkled. We walked upstream to the road above the yard and looked at it, then walked downstream to the edge of the garden and looked at it. We saw nothing we weren't prideful about.[24]

He went off in our old Pontiac and returned in a half hour. He parked in the driveway and got out.

---

[19]elaborate: fancy
[20]latticework: open frame of woven pieces of wood
[21]locust piers: locust-wood supporting poles
[22]cluck: clicking sound
[23]plaster lathe: plaster-covered wooden strips
[24]prideful about: proud of

"Come here," he said. We sat in the grass on the shoulder of the culvert[25] at the edge of the road. "I've been to the store," he said. He pulled a brown paper sack from his pocket. Inside I found ten thimble-shaped chocolate mints, my favorite. From another pocket he produced a rolled band of bright red silk.

"Thank you," I said. "What's that?"

"We want her to know it's a present, don't we? So we've got to tie a ribbon on it. We'll put it right there in the middle of the handrail." He spooled off two yards of ribbon and cut it up with his pocket knife. "Have to make a big one so she can see it from up here in the road."

I chewed a mint and observed his thick horny fingers with the red silk.

It was not to be. Though I was convinced that my father could design and build whatever he wished—the Brooklyn Bridge, the Taj Mahal[26]—he could not tie a bow in the broad ribbon. The silk crinkled and knotted and slipped loose; it simply would not behave. He growled in low tones like a bear trying to dislodge[27] a groundhog from its hole. "I don't know what's the matter with this stuff," he said.

Over the low mumble of his words I heard a different rumble, a gurgle as of pebbles pouring into a broad still pool. "What's that?" I asked.

"What's what?"

"What's that noise?"

He stopped ruining the ribbon and sat still as the sound grew louder. Then his face darkened and veins

---

[25]culvert: underground drainpipe
[26]Taj Mahal: large, elaborate tomb in India
[27]dislodge: remove

stood out in his neck and forehead. His voice was quiet and level now. "Those bastards."

"Who?"

"Those Challenger Paper guys. They've opened the floodgates."[28]

We scrambled up the shoulder into the road.

As the sound got louder it discomposed[29] into many sounds: lappings, bubblings, rippings, undersucks, and splashovers. Almost as soon as we saw the gray-brown thrust of water emerge[30] from beneath the overhanging plum tree, we felt the tremor[31] as it slammed against the culvert, leaping up the shoulder and rolling back. On the yard side it shot out of the culvert as out of a hose. In a few seconds it had overflowed the low creek banks and streamed gray-green along the edge of the yard, furling[32] white around the willow trunks. Debris[33]—black sticks and leaves and grasses—spun on top of the water, and the gullet[34] of the culvert rattled with rolling pebbles.

Our sparkling white bridge was soiled with mud and slimy grasses. The water driving into it reached a gray arm high into the air and slapped down. My father and I watched the hateful battering of our work, our hands in our pockets. He still held the red ribbon and it trickled out his pocket down his trouser leg. The little bridge trembled and began to shake. There was one moment when it sat quite still, as if it had gathered resolve[35] and was fighting back.

---

[28] floodgates: gates for releasing water
[29] discomposed: came apart
[30] emerge: come out
[31] tremor: shaking
[32] furling: curling
[33] debris: ruins
[34] gullet: throat
[35] gathered resolve: stopped to collect itself

And then on the yard side it wrenched[36] away from the log piers, and when that side headed downstream the other side tore away too, and we had a brief glimpse of the bridge parallel in the stream like a strange boat and saw the furthest advance of the floor framed in the quaint[37] lattice arch. The bridge twirled about and the corners caught against both banks and it went over on its side, throwing up the naked underside of the plants like a barn door blown shut. Water piled up behind this damming and finally poured over and around it, eating at the borders of the garden and lawn.

My father kept saying over and over, "Bastards bastards bastards. It's against the law for them to do that."

Then he fell silent.

I don't know how long we stared downstream before we were aware that my mother had arrived. When he first saw her she had already got out of the taxi, which sat idling in the road. She looked good to me, wearing a dress I had never seen, and a strange expression—half amused, half vexed[38]—crossed her face. She looked at us as if she'd caught us doing something naughty.

My father turned to her and tried to speak. "Bastards" was the only word he got out. He choked and his face and neck went dark again. He gestured toward the swamped bridge and the red ribbon fluttered in his fingers.

She looked where he pointed and, as I watched, understanding came into her face, little by little. When she turned again to face us she looked as if she

---

[36]wrenched: violently pulled
[37]quaint: old-fashioned
[38]vexed: annoyed

were in pain. A single tear glistened on her cheek, silver in the cheerful light of midafternoon.

My father dropped his hand and the ribbon fluttered and trailed in the mud.

The tear on my mother's cheek got larger and larger. It detached from her face and became a shiny globe, widening outward like an inflating balloon. At first the tear floated in the air between them, but as it expanded it took my mother and father into itself. I saw them suspended, separate but beginning to drift slowly toward one another. Then my mother looked past my father's shoulder, looked through the bright skin of the tear, at me. The tear enlarged until at last it took me in too. It was warm and salt. As soon as I got used to the strange light inside the tear, I began to swim clumsily toward my parents.

REFLECT ·

Why do you think Donald Kopp took the time to write to Sarah Meyers ("Above and Beyond")? How do you think she felt when she received his letter?

What meaning did the items in the bag have for Molly Fulghum ("The Good Stuff")? For her father?

What acts of kindness and love are described in "Grandma Hattie"?

Describe the relationship between the father and son in "The Overspill." What kind of relationship do you think the father had with the mother?

How is Grandma Hattie's unselfishness toward the homeless different from the acts of kindness and love in the other three readings?

WRITE ·

If you were to put together a bag of items you treasure, what would go into it? Why?

Describe an act of kindness that touched you.

Bob Greene is known for writing human-interest stories. Rather than just reporting facts, this type of story shows how people think, feel, and act. Imagine that you are a newspaper reporter, and write a human-interest story about the events in "The Overspill." Describe what happened, and interview the people involved.

It's hard to imagine buying the weekly groceries without a shopping cart. But it is actually a fairly recent invention.

WHERE DID IT COME FROM?

Have you ever looked at some common, everyday object—like a paper clip or a felt tip pen—and said to yourself, Hmm . . . I wonder who thought that up? Most of us are familiar with the stories behind inventions like the light bulb and the telephone. But many of us have no idea who created some of the small, simple things we use every day. For example, do you know who invented the zipper or the safety pin—two things that keep our world from falling apart?

The following readings tell the story behind the invention of four things you have probably bought or used: the supermarket shopping cart, chewing gum, Velcro fasteners, and perhaps the best-known soft drink in all the world.

As you read each piece, think about how your life would be different if the product had not been invented. Ask yourself, In what ways is the discovery or creation of this invention like the others? In what ways is it different? Was the invention created by accident, or was it planned and developed over time?

Vince Staten's book Can You Trust a
Tomato in January? *is a funny, fact-
filled description of his weekly trip to the
supermarket. As his wife, Judy, takes a
product off the shelf, Staten tells about
its ingredients and history. In the following reading, Staten gives a brief history
of the shopping cart they push around
the store. As you will see, the modern
supermarket shopping cart has come a
long way from the first model.*

The Shopping Cart

From *Can You Trust a Tomato in January?*
Vince Staten

We take the grocery cart for granted. But supermarkets wouldn't be supermarkets if it weren't for
these large, convenient mobile market baskets that
make extended[1] shopping trips possible—just the
sort of experience the supermarket is all about. The
Edison of the aisles,[2] the man who invented the shopping cart, was an Oklahoma greengrocer.[3] One day in
1936 Sylvan Goldman, owner of the Standard and the
Humpty-Dumpty supermarkets in Oklahoma City,
noticed that his customers quit shopping as soon as
their wicker baskets got too full or got too heavy for
them to carry.

What to do?

---

[1] extended: longer
[2] Edison of the aisles: Thomas Edison; the author is using
 his name as a synonym for "famous inventor"
[3] greengrocer: seller of fruits and vegetables

Goldman had a stroke of genius, an idea that would ensure the future of the supermarket. He scribbled out the plans for his immodestly[4] titled biography,[5] *The Cart That Changed the World*. That wasn't far from wrong. True supermarketing wasn't possible until shoppers could accumulate[6] mounds of groceries.

Sylvan Goldman invented the grocery cart.

The original X-frame model—two shallow wire baskets mounted on wheels—was three feet tall, two feet long, and a foot-and-a-half wide. And it was olive green to match his store's decor. The baskets were removable so the carts could be folded up and stored.

The carts were assembled by Goldman's maintenance man Fred Young. And at first Young and his crew made only enough for Goldman's stores. That's when Goldman had his second brilliant idea. He would patent the design and sell the carts to other stores. Goldman formed the Folding Carrier Company and displayed his invention at the first Super Market Institute Convention in New York in 1937. And did land-office[7] business.

But winning over shoppers was another story. Early supermarket shoppers didn't immediately take to Goldman's new-fangled[8] grocery carts. They preferred the market baskets they had carried from home. It took some persuading to get housewives to walk along pushing these goofy-looking carts. Goldman's solution was to pay his employees' wives to walk around the store filling up carts. Other women

---

[4]immodestly: boastfully
[5]biography: nonfiction book about a person's life
[6]accumulate: gather together
[7]land-office: rapidly growing
[8]new-fangled: modern

saw how convenient it was to have a basket on wheels and pretty soon nobody brought their baskets. By the forties the shopping cart was standard equipment everywhere.

There's been little change since then. The baby seat was added in 1947 with the patented Nest-Baskart, which also had an open bottom shelf and a swinging rear panel to allow carts to be nested and take up less space. About the only modification[9] since then was that little ad on the front of the cart. ActMedia of Darien, Connecticut, pioneered the practice of attaching these junior billboards to shopping carts in 1972. They didn't arrive in our Winn-Dixie[10] until four years ago.

For shoppers the grocery cart is a constant companion from the time they enter the store until they drive out of the parking lot. Some carts have also found their way past the parking lot. A few wind up as laundry carts, go-carts, walkers, even barbecue grills. The average supermarket loses 12 percent of its carts a year to theft. Another 17 percent simply wear out. So, at the average rate of $100 per pop, for a large store that can add up to $5,000 a year to the cost of staying open.

---

[9] modification: change
[10] Winn-Dixie: name of a grocery store

WHERE DID IT COME FROM? 79 · · · · · · · · · · ·

How long would you guess people have been chewing gum? Fifty years? A hundred? Guess again. It is also part of life in many different countries, not just the United States. Whether you love it or hate it, chewing gum is here to stay.

Chewing Gum

In *The Invention of Ordinary Things*
Don L. Wulffson

Believe it or not, people have been chewing gum for centuries. The Mayans and other Central Americans chewed chicle, a hardened juice that comes from the sapodilla tree. The people of Asia and Africa chewed wads of grass, leaves, or tree sap for relaxation and enjoyment. The Indians of North America were fond of spruce resin, a chewy substance found in local trees.

When the colonists came to America, they were surprised to see the Indians chewing gum. At first the colonists made fun of the Indians, and thought the habit of chomping on wads of sap was strange and silly. In time, however, the colonists tried the stuff themselves, realized what they had been missing, and were soon out-chewing and out-chomping the native Americans.

In the early 1800s the first shop for making and selling chewing gum came into being. The shop sold pine gum—the same stuff the Indians had been getting for free for hundreds of years.

Soon, more gum shops and factories began popping up. Most of these produced spruce gum; others offered a type of gum made from paraffin.[1]

The kind of gum that people around the world chew today is not made from spruce resin or paraffin. It is made from chicle, the tree juice known to the people of Central America for centuries.

In the year 1870 a photographer by the name of Charles Adams was experimenting with chicle as a substitute for rubber. Adams wanted to make goods such as toys, masks, and rain boots out of chicle, but every experiment failed. Sitting in his workshop one day, tired and discouraged, he popped a piece of his surplus stock[2] into his mouth. As he sat chewing away, the idea suddenly came to him to add flavoring to the chicle and sell it as gum. Twenty years later Adams was a rich man, the owner and manager of a giant chewing-gum factory.

Gum caught on quickly with the American people. Many doctors of the time, however, decided that the rubbery stuff was dangerous to health. For example, in 1869 one physician wrote an article warning that the chewing of gum "would exhaust the salivary glands[3] and cause the intestines to stick together."

In spite of such warnings, the use of chewing gum in the United States has increased rapidly over the years. For example, in 1914 the average American chewed thirty-nine sticks a year; at present the number is almost two hundred sticks a year, and is still on the rise.

---

[1] paraffin: waxy substance used to make candles
[2] surplus stock: extra supply
[3] salivary glands: glands that secrete moisture into the mouth

According to some psychologists, one reason people chew more gum today is that they are more nervous than the people of the past. One basis for this claim is that every time a war breaks out (something which, quite naturally, makes people very nervous), gum sales around the world immediately skyrocket.

As you can see in any drugstore or supermarket, the production of chewing gum has kept right in step with the ever-growing demand. One estimate has it that almost twenty-four million miles of chewing gum roll out of U.S. factories every year.

Velcro is the "sticky stuff on strips" that is used to fasten gym shoes, jackets, and other articles of clothing. Think for a minute. How many pieces of clothing with Velcro do you own? As you will find out in this selection, Velcro is a fairly new product that became popular very quickly.

Velcro: Improving on Nature

In *They All Laughed . . .*
Ira Flatow

When astronauts and cosmonauts[1] first began circling the globe, they faced a unique[2] problem: how to keep track of all their stuff. On the ground, if you wanted to stow your car keys, for example, you simply left them on the night table. They could be found in the morning right where you left them—perhaps after a bit of last-minute searching on the way out the door—but at least they stayed put.

Space travelers faced a different problem. Objects had a habit of just floating off. A pencil, a wrench, would just hang around drifting weightlessly wherever a tiny shove or air current would take it.

Keeping tabs on a capsule full of flotsam[3] was a job in itself, a full-time job because if a tiny piece lodged itself into the hardware, it could short-circuit who-knows-what. The fact that orbital living quarters[4]

---

[1] cosmonauts: astronauts of the former Soviet Union
[2] unique: one of a kind
[3] flotsam: drifting objects
[4] orbital living quarters: living quarters in a spaceship

would make a phone booth look spacious only compounded[5] the problem of keeping things neat and
orderly.

How could one make sure things stayed put?

The answer came from a lucky walk in the country taken just a few years before the space race began
in the early 1950s. Our hero was one George de Mestral, who happened to be taking a stroll one day in
his native Switzerland.

Upon arriving home, he found his jacket covered
with cockleburs. Picking the sticky seed pods off his
clothing, de Mestral wondered what act of natural
engineering could account for their tenacious[6] sticking ability. Whereas you or I might just curse the
darned cockleburs for being such a nuisance,[7] de
Mestral pulled out his microscope and took a careful
look. Focusing in on the cockleburs' structure, he
noticed they were covered with little hooks that
entangled[8] themselves in the loops of fabric of the
jacket. Mother Nature had invented an ingenious
method for catching a free ride to the next seeding
spot by lodging[9] her seed carriers in the fur of pass-
ing birds and animals.

If nature could be so resourceful,[10] why not take
advantage of her design and turn nuisance into neces-
sity? Artificially create a system of hooks and loops
that when pressed together tightly stick to one
another but when pried[11] apart easily separate. Velcro—derived from *vel*vet and *cro*chet—was first

---

[5]compounded: increased
[6]tenacious: stubborn
[7]nuisance: bother
[8]entangled: caught
[9]lodging: sticking
[10]resourceful: clever
[11]pried: pulled

made in France. Each Velcro tape was made by hand and took almost forever to produce. The loops could be easily made by machine but the hooks did not lend themselves easily to mechanization. What to do? Make the loops mechanically and then cut them in such a way that the clipped ends formed hooks! This way hooks could be fashioned from loops from the simple act of cutting.

With the mechanical problems solved, Velcro's holding power was improved. The original nylon material used to make the hooks and loops was strengthened by thickening. Blends of polyester and nylon made them even stronger. NASA found ribbons of unique fastening material it needed to hold the countless odds and ends of space travel.

Even today, no better substitute has been found. When getting ready to leave orbit, space shuttle astronauts literally spend a full day in space collecting all of the material Velcroed to the walls.

Of course Velcro has been improved over the years. It has become impervious to[12] water, chemicals, and corrosive[13] ultraviolet light.[14] Extra-strong Velcro can be made out of stainless steel and synthetic fibers that withstand temperatures upwards of 800°F. and do not catch fire.

---

[12]impervious to: unable to be penetrated by
[13]corrosive: damaging
[14]ultraviolet light: light at wavelengths above the range of human eyesight

A pick-me-up is something that gives a person a burst of energy, like coffee or tea. There is another popular pick-me-up, a soft drink that is known all around the world. The following reading tells how this well-known drink came about almost by accident.

Dr. Pemberton's Pick-Me-Up

In *Paul Harvey's the Rest of the Story*
Paul Aurandt

In the first place, Dr. Pemberton wasn't even a doctor. But who'd trust a product called "Mr. Pemberton's Triplex Liver Pills"?

No one.

Therefore he called it "Dr. Pemberton's Globe of Flower Cough Syrup" and "Dr. Pemberton's Extract of Styllinger Blood Medicine."

But if Dr. Pemberton wasn't a doctor, he also wasn't a quack.[1] He merely lived in an era, right after the Civil War, when the corner druggist knew as much about medicines as the national drug manufacturers. And that's just what John Pemberton was. A corner druggist.

It was sometime after moving his business from Columbus to Atlanta—some while after "Dr. Pemberton's Indian Queen Hair Dye"—that this obscure[2] Georgia pharmacist[3] started fiddling[4] with a basement brew you'll want to know about.

---

[1] quack: incompetent doctor
[2] obscure: little-known
[3] pharmacist: druggist
[4] fiddling: experimenting

Most patent medicines[5] in those days contained alcohol. None of that in John Pemberton's new concoction.[6] In fact, according to some, he was trying to effect a headache cure . . . or perhaps a hangover cure for the other patent medicines.

John experimented with the extracts of fruits and nuts and leaves, but that was for taste. If he was going to cure a headache he'd need, perhaps, a stimulant?[7] Yes. Caffeine. And an analgesic.[8] Some say . . . cocaine.

Now it was all over but the selling. But John, who had spent most of his time developing this new pick-me-up, would need financial help. So, during the summer of 1886, Dr. Pemberton took a jug of the reddish-brown syrup to Jacobs Pharmacy, one of the most reputable in Atlanta.

What was in it, the manager wanted to know?

Dr. Pemberton explained that it was a secret but the manager should try some. Just mix with water and drink.

Well, Jacobs bought Pemberton's potion . . . advertised it, too . . . but sales were slow. Apparently Georgians were quite free of aches and pains that summer. That's when fate stumbled in.

The story goes that a customer came into the pharmacy one morning with a hangover. The clerk remembered Dr. Pemberton's syrup and went to mix some. He was new on the job, not yet acquainted with the procedure . . . and used carbonated water by mistake.

---

[5] patent medicines: over-the-counter medicine
[6] concoction: mixture
[7] stimulant: something that energizes
[8] analgesic: pain killer

His mistake is still in the recipe today. Any cocaine in the original creation has long since been eliminated,[9] so it may or may not cure your headache. The other ingredients remain basically the same.

Dr. Pemberton, the master of cures, could not cure himself. His health failed soon after that last discovery. The little business he built around it could have been bought for less than two thousand dollars when he died.

So the country druggist never shared the pot of gold at the end of what is now a rainbow of lights as wide as the world—spelling out . . . Coca-Cola!

---

[9] eliminated: omitted; left out

REFLECT ·······································

Why do you think shoppers at first hesitated to use Sylvan Goldman's shopping carts? What made shoppers change their minds?

Why does the author of "Dr. Pemberton's Pick-Me-Up" keep the name of the product a secret until the last line of the story? Would you have enjoyed the article more if you had known from the start that it was about Coca-Cola? Why or why not?

Which of the four inventions were the result of planning? Which were accidents?

In your opinion, which of the four inventions described in this unit has had the most far-reaching effects?

WRITE ·

Imagine that you are a regular shopper at Sylvan
Goldman's store in 1936. Write a letter to a friend in
another town describing the new shopping carts and
telling why you think they are a good—or a bad—
idea.

If you could invent something to make life easier or
more fun, what would it be? Let your imagination go,
and write a description of what your invention does
and how it works.

The design of the original shopping cart has changed
very little over the years. Think of something that
could be done to make the cart even more useful or
easier to use. Write a description of your changes,
and explain why shopping-cart makers should adopt
your idea.

There isn't much difference between one brand of
chewing gum or soft drink and another; yet there are
many different brands being successfully sold to the
public. Make up a new brand of gum or soft drink,
and write an ad for it. Tell people why your brand is
unique or better than all the others.

Louie Anderson is a popular figure on TV and in comedy clubs across the nation. To rise to the top, he had to overcome many obstacles.

TURNING POINTS

If you're like most people, you've experienced many turning points—moments when a decision or action changed your life. Maybe you decided to go back to school or find a new job. You may have discovered that you have a special skill or talent. Or perhaps you had an experience that made you realize life is more surprising or strange or beautiful than you ever imagined. What important turning points have marked your life so far?

The people in the following readings made decisions that sent them down new paths in life. As their stories show, all of life's turning points are not pleasant. But as these people learned, even a painful experience can have a positive effect.

As you read, ask yourself, If this person had a chance to live life over, would he or she do things differently? What would this person's life be like if the turning point hadn't occurred?

Eula Lee Maddox grew up in a family of sharecroppers—people who farm rented land, turning over part of their crops as rent to the landowners. In spite of her difficult childhood, Maddox educated herself and went on to enjoy a successful career in publishing. In the following piece, Maddox talks about a time that she stood up for herself. This turning point, she says, gave her the pride and strength she needed to succeed in life.

Words in a Blue Notebook

In *Legacies*
Eula Lee Maddox

I was six years old, a dirty, barefoot child patting out make-believe tea cakes from mud in the yard of the sharecropper shack where I lived with my father, my two sisters, and my grandmother. I was eating my biggest tea cake when the landowner and his hunting friends came across the field, stopped about twenty feet away, and started talking about me as if I were a dead dove or a shot quail.[1]

"What is it?"

"Jesus, it's eating dirt. It lives in that?"

"Hey now, I know," the landowner said. "A curse. Trash. The South's disgrace."

I quit chewing and grabbed up my mud tea cakes with both hands and slammed them at the men's faces.

---

[1]quail: type of bird

"I am not so a curse and trash and the South's disgrace," I said, "and I ain't no it. I am me."

The landowner swore at me and said if I didn't cut it out he'd give me a whipping. The others laughed. One ran over and dropped a dollar bill in front of me. I snatched up the dollar, wrapped it in soupy mud, and hit him between the eyes with it.

They walked away laughing.

The next year I started first grade and learned to read and write. "I am me" was the first sentence I wrote on my own. At the end of second grade my teacher gave me a little blue notebook "for making A-plus on all your work."

I wrote my name on the blue cover, found the words "curse," "trash," and "disgrace" in the teacher's *Dictionary for Children*, and copied the definitions on the first page of my blue notebook. On the inside cover I printed in big capital letters, "I AM NOT A CURSE. I AM NOT TRASH. I AM NOT THE SOUTH'S DISGRACE. I AM ME."

Every day through grade school and high school I kept the blue notebook near me, usually in the bottom of the book bag my grandmother made me from leftover quilt scraps. Anytime I was tempted to slack[2] an assignment, I'd see my words on its inside cover and I'd see the landowner and his friends laughing at me.

By the time I was a sophomore in high school I was on fire with the dream of going to college even though I knew it was impossible. I filled all the blue notebook's pages with outlines of college courses, clothes I'd wear there, even friends I'd make.

A week after graduation I found work as a sales-clerk thirty miles away. I packed my few clothes in

---

[2] slack: do in a lazy or careless way

my book bag, wrapped the blue notebook in a square of sacking cloth,[3] tied it with heavy cord, and asked my grandmother and my sisters to "keep this bundle for me till I get settled."

The next year my grandmother died, and shortly thereafter I found a job on a college campus five states away that allowed me to take two free classes each semester. I'd send for the bundle, I wrote my father and sisters, soon as I got settled.

Eventually, I knew I was as settled as I'd ever be. I asked my sisters about my bundle. Neither could remember it. I took a week off and went back and searched the rubble[4] of all the sharecropper shacks we'd lived in, but I found nothing remotely akin[5] to my blue notebook.

Never mind. I'll always see my words on the inside cover of the blue notebook as clearly as the day I wrote them. Then as now, I am me.

---

[3] sacking cloth: coarse fabric used to make sacks
[4] rubble: broken pieces
[5] remotely akin: in any way similar

When her husband died, Alice Lindberg Snyder was deeply shaken. To cope with her loss, Snyder went through counseling. This experience helped her discover talents and needs she didn't know she had. Though in her seventies, she learned to live each day to the fullest.

from *Freedom*

In *Gifts of Age*
Charlotte Painter

The tap shoes[1] she wanted were in the window of the Children's Bootery, so she went inside and asked for them. The salesman raised his eyebrows but lifted her foot onto his metal measure, out of habit maybe. She told him her size, said it hadn't changed in sixty years. Nice that they measure the children's feet every time, she thought, but this was her second childhood, not her first. "You been dancing that long too?" the young man asked.

"Just started," she said. Had a talent for it too, but she didn't boast.[2] Actually, she did dance as a child and had had a few more lessons lately. The shoes were a must now, especially since Edie's call.

"You'd better come on and visit now, Alice. You're going to get old. You're going to die like everybody else, so *do it now!*" By most standards she was ancient already. So *now* was the time.

All those things she hadn't done when Bill was alive she had begun to do now just because they

---

[1]tap shoes: shoes with metal heels and tips for tap dancing
[2]boast: brag

were in her, the perfectly harmless things she had done as a young girl: sailing, swimming, whistling, tap-dancing. That fun-loving nature of her childhood hadn't died; she just hadn't turned it loose all those years. Now it was taking over. Let other people worry about brittle bones if they wanted to—that was their lookout. Or the impropriety of an old woman who sticks her fingers between her teeth to hail a cab. Let them think her a zany eccentric if they liked. She was through with neglecting the part of herself that wanted to play.

She was thinking of taking her grandson rafting on the Rogue River with a friend of his. Better not wait on that. And of going with Edie to the Hebrides to hear the wind shriek in their ears.

"Do you think it's unusual for someone my age to tap?" she asked the shoe salesman.

"Unusual but okay by me," the salesman grinned and tied the bow on the tap shoes for her. "How about a demonstration?"

"Move that stool aside," she said. "I'll show you something right here." Still sitting in her chair, she let her feet beat a quick rhythm on the vinyl floor and hummed "The Sidewalks of New York." The salesman was impressed. "You see, it'd be great therapy for somebody in a wheelchair. Anyone can learn to tap-dance."

The salesman wrapped up the shoes. "And I'll have one of those balloons you give away too, please," she said.

Alice was into taboo-busting. She wasn't going to sit back and be the widow of a university professor who limited herself to activity suitable to her years and status. She had poured at her last faculty tea. Now she was going to become all that she could be.

Funnyman Louie Anderson has appeared in many clubs and on many TV shows. People who know him only as a comic may be surprised to hear that he had a very unhappy childhood. Anderson was one of eleven children in a family ruled by an alcoholic father.

In his book Dear Dad, *Anderson tries to make sense of his life by writing letters to his father, who has been dead for many years. The letters describe Anderson's fear and confusion. But they also describe the forgiveness and love he came to feel toward his dad. In the letter that follows, Anderson talks about a turning point he had in high school.*

And I Never Did

In *Dear Dad*
Louie Anderson

Dear Dad,

It's ironic that a kid who quit high school would be asked back to give a motivational speech, but that's exactly the invitation I received the other day. I never felt much a part of any school I attended, high school most of all. My weight was the trouble. When you're fat, you're excluded from the various social groups. I think one of the reasons my joke about carrying a nine-by-twelve rug to nursery school goes over so well is that everyone carries some kind of burden in life.

In high school I was a hippie. I had long hair and did whatever I could to buck the norm.[1] I was a radical[2] looking for trouble. I once got in trouble for refusing to stand during the national anthem. I didn't do it because I had anything against the U.S. After all, my father was a veteran. I did it to irritate this one teacher who was a real stiff rod. That and my fondness for antagonizing[3] authority.

This teacher was a real rigid goofball, and when I refused to stand, he hauled my butt down to the assistant principal's office and started to spew[4] out this patriotic nonsense about his being a veteran who didn't risk his life so some anti-American commie[5] punk like myself could desecrate[6] the flag. That got me to spouting off about your being a disabled veteran. We yelled at each other for about fifteen minutes, while the assistant VP, a short, squat man with a bald head shaped like a nosecone, watched with his feet propped on his desk. When we finished yelling, he told us both to get out.

However, it was gym class that accelerated[7] the end of my education. I hated, absolutely *hated*, gym class. Undressing my fat body in the locker room was the worst ego-shattering[8] experience of my teenage life. If the kids weren't cracking jokes about my weight, they were staring at me. Some weren't as obvious as others. But I knew that they wanted to see what someone as fat as me looked like. It's the same way people look at someone who's missing a limb.

---

[1]buck the norm: break the rules
[2]radical: rebel
[3]antagonizing: angering
[4]spew: spit
[5]commie: Communist
[6]desecrate: dishonor
[7]accelerated: speeded up
[8]ego-shattering: confidence-destroying

People freak at anything that deviates[9] from the norm. These days especially, they treat fat like a disease, like they'll catch it if they get too close.

While changing clothes, my heart would pound so hard waiting for the first giggle, trying to cover myself until I could get the undersized gym shorts on. I'd burn from embarrassment, feeling the blood flush my skin. Then I'd have to trot out onto the field, usually arriving late, where this sadistic[10] little gym teacher with a big, bushy mustache and bowed legs would make me run and jump when all I wanted to do was hide.

The coach, as he liked to be called, always had this idea that he could take a guy who had been fat for ten years—me, for instance—and slim him down in ten months. I hated him for that, but I hated myself more.

It got to the point where I would do anything to get out of gym, including skipping the entire day of school. All I could think about was this one horrible hour. It filled me with so much fear and anxiety that I couldn't cope with the other hours in the day. As such, going to school became unbearable. Finally, I knew it had to end. I couldn't continue living with this stress. Then one day the twerp with the whistle roared the three words I dreaded.

"Take a lap!"

"Oh no, not laps," I thought.

I hated laps. I couldn't do them. I was fat. I smoked. I wasn't interested. I didn't want to do them. I'd walk.

"Pick it up, Anderson!" he'd shout. "Move it!"

---

[9]deviates: differs from
[10]sadistic: cruel

"Screw him," I thought. And one day I just refused to do it.

"No," I thought, "I'm not going to run the lap."

Coach asked me what I was doing.

"I'm not going to run the lap," I explained calmly. "I can't, and you can't make me."

It wasn't very dramatic, at least as dramatic moments go, but the mini-mutiny[11] I staged had a lasting effect on me. I was immediately ordered to get dressed and told to report to the chief gym czar,[12] an even more demented, disagreeable fellow. I got dressed and walked out the door.

However, instead of going into the gym office, I turned the other way and walked right off the school grounds. "You know," I thought, "I'm never going to come back here."

Signed,

And I never did

---

[11]mini-mutiny: small rebellion
[12]czar: leader

Penny Longworth has had many difficul-
ties to overcome. As a child, she was
abused by her father. At the age of nine-
teen, she became a teenage mother. She
married the father, and a second child
soon followed. Longworth's husband
turned out to be even more abusive than
her father had been. She stayed in the
marriage until her daughters were
grown. Then, in a major turning point
in her life, she struck out on her own.

from *Me and the Guy Upstairs*[1]

In *No More Frogs, No More Princes*
Penny Longworth

I was raised to believe the man is the head of the household, but I just felt he was taking over too much of me, and my mind was not going to go. I wouldn't let it. Maybe it was my mother in me. My mother went through a rather abusive life, and she survived it. Her mother had her last baby the day after her father was buried, so my mother had a rough life. Maybe it was something she taught me or something she told me. I don't know.

I got to the point where I was contemplating suicide. I thought about jumping over the banister.[2] Then I got to thinking about how nice that hemlock[3] hedge would look in his Italian seasoning. And then I thought, no, you can't do that. You wouldn't have freedom then. Before I do something stupid, I

---

[1] guy upstairs: God
[2] banister: railing on a staircase
[3] hemlock: poisonous plant

thought, I'd better get out. I didn't want to end up in solitary[4] some place. And I'd probably mess up suicide and cripple myself, and then I'd really be locked in there. So I left.

I moved out the day after Christmas in '90. I moved out right in front of him. He sat in the staircase and watched me take my stuff out the front door. He said I'd be a bag lady. He said, "You'll never amount to anything, nobody's going to take pity on you, nobody's going to feed you. You're worthless, you don't have no brains, you're not capable of taking care of yourself."

Yeah, I was afraid. But I didn't bring the kids with me this time, they were grown, and that helped. My youngest one told me I deserted her, but she was twenty-one when I left. My other one was married.

It helped to know that welfare was there, that Womenhelp [a community program for women in transition[5]] was there. I went to live with my sister first because Womenhelp has a rule that you have to live away from your husband for two weeks on your own before you can go into a safe house. I have two sisters. One has a husband, and one is a widow. In the daytime, I stayed at the sister's with a husband. When he came home in the night, I'd sleep at the widow's house, so that way I didn't mess up my sister's marriage by moving in. I had my stuff all in her basement, but I wasn't there.

Shirley, my Womenhelp counselor, pretty much put the backbone into my ideas. I knew what I wanted to do, but I wasn't real sure I could accomplish it, and she gave me the confidence that I could do it.

---

[4] end up in solitary: land in jail
[5] in transition: in a period of change

I took my GED test[6] in April of '91, and I passed it. I needed a 225, and I got a 263. I'm a lot freer and happier. I'm able to think and buy what groceries I want to buy, and I've got running water and a bathroom now. [She laughs heartily.]

I did career testing, too. My father and husband had told me that I didn't have a brain, that I was worthless, but the career testing and the GED showed me that I had a brain.

I tested in that career test above ninety in everything but science, and I was above eighty in that. I was just above average in science, and way above average in all the other subjects. Communications and business was my strongest ones. I chose communications. It was like a sixth sense in my life all along, instinct, woman's intuition. I'm headed for college in the fall. I'm happier than a lark right now. I have no problems. Just if my grants[7] for college come through. But when my grants come through, my assistance is going to be shut off and my food stamps. If you go to college, they take it away. If I have a choice of assistance or college, I'd be stupid not to choose college because, on down the road, I can get my bachelor's or my master's. I'll try my bachelor's first, and I'll go from there.

I want to write a novel about my life, and I think I need a little more up here [she points to her head] before I can get it right. I've got the story up there, but I've got to get it out on paper. Maybe I'll start a magazine or my own publishing company or something. What's to stop me? I'm in control.

I wonder how I'm going to get my room and board paid for after September 1, but there's food

---

[6] GED test: high school equivalency examination
[7] grants: sums of money

banks. I'll get a job or something. I'm going to take a
civil-service test to be a houseparent at the college.
I'm also checking with cerebral palsy to see if they
need anybody to stay with someone on a weekend
when their regular help is off. I can handle that kind
of work. I can cope. I think the Guy Upstairs will
take care of me. After what I've been through, He's
going to let me starve to death? Get real! [She
laughs.]

I'm working on a quilt to sell, too. It's all hand-
made. I have a sewing machine, but I don't use it.
They said I could get a lot for the quilt. I've been at it
since the first of the year. I make my own binding,[8]
too. If I can get $500 for it, I can buy a car to get
around town in.

[She opens up an album on her coffee table. It is
filled with pictures of quilts she has made.] That's my
granddaughter's baby quilt. I hand appliqued[9] that
one. That's a double wedding band quilt. It's all hand
pieced and appliqued onto a black sheet. It took me
two years to make that. I made one they raffled off
for $600 for the high school band. It has musical
notes and instruments and the bull dog motto for the
school.

Making quilts has always been my escape. I
pretty much think quilting was born in me, you
know. My grandmother and my great-grandmother
were always quilting and putting pieces together. It
just seemed to come natural. It was something born
in me. I take regular patterns and change them to suit
myself.

I don't need a man. I need a degree. I got to
write my book. I don't drink, but I go to the club

---

[8]binding: edging
[9]appliqued: sewed on fabric cut-outs to create a picture

every Friday and Saturday night, and I dance with whoever's there. I'm forty-five and still able to produce, and the thirty-five-year-olds are coming on to me. And I'm saying, get out of my face, boy, I've got plans. I don't need you.

I was about two hundred pounds when I left him. I'm down to 180 now. I thought my shape would turn away the men, but I'm telling you the young ones are coming on to me quicker than the old ones. I was out with a twenty-seven-year-old last night. He took me to his place and cooked me a steak and baked potato with a tossed salad. He taught me how to play pool. He took me back home, and he gave me a nice hug and a peck on the cheek. I love it.

You got to look for the good things in life. Like the little mother bird feeding her babies. You look out your window, and how many shades of green do you see in the woods? How many shades of blue are in the sky in the day? How many times does the moon change its color in a month? It's never the same. You can find beauty if you look for it. You got to look for something.

You have to laugh, you have to have a positive attitude, too. People can give you advice, but you got to do it. You got to do it yourself. They can hold your hand, give you a room and feed you, but the bottom line is you got to do it yourself. You got to get your mind on doing it, doing what you want.

REFLECT ·

What turning point in the life of Eula Lee Maddox is described in "Words in a Blue Notebook"?

If you could use only one word to describe Maddox, what would it be? Why?

What turning point in the life of Alice Lindberg Snyder does the reading "Freedom" describe?

How do you feel about Snyder's decision to learn how to tap-dance despite being in her seventies? Why do you feel as you do?

Do you think Louie Anderson ("And I Never Did") would have finished high school if he hadn't had such a bad experience in gym class? Why or why not?

What is Penny Longworth's attitude toward life in "Me and the Guy Upstairs"? What do you think made her develop this attitude?

Both Eula Lee Maddox and Louie Anderson stood up to authority figures. What do Alice Lindberg Snyder and Penny Longworth have in common?

WRITE ··································

Reread what Eula Lee Maddox wrote in the front of her blue notebook. Then write a few sentences of your own that define who you are and what you want to become.

Louie Anderson wrote letters to his father, even though he was no longer alive to read them. Write a letter to a friend or loved one who has passed away. Tell this person about some recent event in your life, how you feel about it, and how you think this person would have reacted.

Write a short play about the day Penny Longworth left her husband. Include a conversation between Penny, her husband, and the twenty-one-year-old daughter. Give directions on where the conversation should take place and how each person should say his or her lines.

More and more women are taking jobs that once were reserved for men only. The sight of a woman in a hard hat no longer raises eyebrows.

Trading Places

Have you ever wondered what it would be like to trade your present life for a completely different one? Perhaps you've wondered what it would be like to have been born in a different family, in a different part of the country, or in a different part of the world. Or maybe you've just daydreamed about leaving everything behind and starting fresh someplace else. If you've ever had thoughts like these, what caused them? What did you imagine your new life would have that your present life does not?

Each of the people in the readings that follow traded their place in life for something completely new and different. Some returned to their old way of life. One left it forever.

As you read, think about whether each person successfully made the trade. Ask yourself why the person wanted to trade places and whether you can imagine yourself doing the same.

John Coleman, president of Haverford College, was sorry that his job kept him from experiencing everyday life. To get a new point of view, he decided to take a break from his presidency and travel around the country, working at simple laboring jobs a few weeks at a time. He told no one about his background.

Coleman wrote down his experiences in a diary that was later published. The following reading is from this journal.

Wednesday, February 28

In *Blue Collar Journal*
John Coleman

A full day laying more of the storm sewer. This time we were without Gus.

The coverup code for sloppy workmanship is complex here. The tests of whether we are laying a good storm sewer or not are the slope of the line[1] and the tightness of the joints. There is no faking it in the slope. The county inspectors have the same laser beams we do; all they have to do is shoot the beam through from the bottom of one manhole to the next one to tell if we did our job right. The joints are something else again. Sometimes the pieces fit together easily, and sometimes they never quite mesh. The crew on the line hurries to cover as many of the joints as possible with a thin layer of dirt before the bosses come along; the joints get buried well before we turn to the rest of the pipe. The bosses then order

---

[1] slope of the line: correct placement of the system of pipes

the poorer fits among those still showing to be covered before the inspector comes along. The inspector
wants the work to pass the test if he likes the contractor, so he looks to get the last of the pipe buried too.

Whatever we have done is soon out of sight. It
just remains to be seen what happens when the first
heavy storms come along. I don't know a good storm
sewer from a bad one. Yet, by and large, I thought we
did honest work today. I can recall one or two joints
that I wish I had done better, but I'm not ashamed of
my work.

Each day I see more clearly how awkward I am
at most jobs requiring the use of tools or equipment.
I didn't drive that truck well (how long has it been
since I used a gearshift at all?). I know now that I
don't use a sledgehammer, a chain saw, a ratchet
wrench, or a pipe cutter very well either. When I was
in high school, my ineptness[2] at athletics was well
known. "We don't want Coleman on our team" were
familiar words to my ears. I half expect to hear them
here in reference to my use of tools. Certainly that
explains why so many orders to me begin, "John, get
a shovel and . . ." That is one tool I use well.

The expectations held out for a laborer are not
high, however. Part of the time it is enough that he
be there, an impersonal item on hand when needed.
A young, arrogant[3] employee of the developer at Pine
Hill illustrated that point today. Some mud splattered
onto his all-too-clean levis as he stood near the ditch.
Noticing it, he reached a hand toward me for my
shovel, scraped the mud off, and returned the shovel,
never once having looked at or spoken to me. The
shovel was there, and that was enough.

---

[2] ineptness: lack of ability
[3] arrogant: overly proud or self-important

Dick, who is normally a decent and warm guy, represented another aspect of this attitude to laborers. He was mad at Stanley, who had forgotten two items when loading the truck back at the trailer today. Gus, being Gus, naturally noticed the mistakes. That brought Dick, as the supervisor for this squad, a dressing down.[4] As he drove me to the job later, Dick said, "What bothers me most is when you rely on a guy like Stanley and he lets you down. He's a pipe man and knows better. If he were just some goddamn laborer, I wouldn't expect anything of him. But he's not."

Just a goddamn laborer. Would I ever get hardened to hearing that if this were my life's work? It is a precondition[5] for loving others that any man love himself first. How can he do that if the part of his life which is his job is treated in so callous[6] a way?

This concern is easy enough for me to feel today because I am just a goddamn laborer for these next weeks. The test is whether I'll feel it when I get back to my regular job. Someday I'll leave Haverford. I'm vain enough that I'll want faculty, students, and board to say at that time that, all things considered, I've done the job well. But it will matter just as much to me to hear men and women in the secretarial posts, housekeeping, buildings, and grounds say that this college treated them with respect.

To the extent that anyone back on the campus feels tonight that he is just a goddamn laborer, we have failed as much as if we cheated him in his pay.

---

[4] dressing down: scolding
[5] precondition: necessary element
[6] callous: unfeeling

Linen Bliss was the daughter of a successful stockbroker. She went to college in the East and was married at nineteen to a Yale graduate. After five years, the marriage ended, and Bliss had a breakdown. To get away from it all, Bliss went on a vacation with her three small children to a ranch in Wyoming. She fell in love with the outdoor life and decided to leave the East for good. She met her present husband, Dave, at a rodeo.

As you read the interview with Bliss, think about the strength of character it took for her to make a complete change in her lifestyle. Do you think she ever doubted herself or wondered if she had made a mistake?

from *Linen Bliss*

In *Cowgirls*
Teresa Jordan

I guess I am a classic case of "dude[1] comes West, meets handsome cowboy, marries handsome cowboy, rides off into the sunset, and lives happily ever after." That has happened many, many times, and it darned sure happened to me.

When Dave and I got married, we didn't have any plumbing or telephone. There were no cattle guards on the road, so we had to open seven gates to

---

[1] dude: city person unfamiliar with outdoor life

get in here. The road was gumbo,[2] and if we had a drop of rain we couldn't get out.

I was on a real pioneer spirit high. Everything we did was the hard way. We were seventy-five miles from the closest town and had so few of the modern conveniences I was used to. I was completely taken up with learning to rough it,[3] and with conquering my new occupation.

It took about four years for me to really feel confident. Those first four years, I still felt like I was kind of intruding[4] on my husband's bachelor life, or perhaps it was more like intruding on a very masculine domain.[5] There were so many things I had to prove to myself as well as him, and I suppose the community. I had to totally divorce myself from all the things I had relied on in the past as being me— my education, or rather schooling, background, "family heritage." If I was going to be a successful western ranch wife, I had to forget everything I was. Of course, it wasn't a successful ranch wife that I had to be. I just had to develop a "me" that was me on my own rather than live up to a pedigree[6] with none of my own signature on it.[7]

I knew little about horses and nothing about cattle. But Dave was great. He expected right from the start that I would learn it, and that I would work with him. It never occurred to him that I wouldn't be able to do it. I was a ranch wife married to him and we were going to do ranch work together, and there was nothing he didn't expect me to do.

---

[2]gumbo: an especially sticky form of mud
[3]rough it: live without modern conveniences
[4]intruding: butting in
[5]domain: kingdom
[6]pedigree: upper-class status one is born into
[7]none of my own signature on it: nothing that reflects what one is really like

As an example, when Scott was five weeks old, Dave went to rope steers at the Denver Stock Show. He drew up badly. He was supposed to rope his first steer on the first day, and his second one ten days later. Then the weather turned and Dave couldn't get back here between the two go-rounds. It was twenty-four degrees below zero, and I had two hundred cows to feed by myself with a five-week-old baby. The only way I could load the hundred-pound sacks of cattle cake onto the tailgate of the pickup was to drop them off the top of the cake pile onto the freezer and then slide them into the truck. Our freezer still has a big dent in the hood. But Dave expected me to handle the situation, and I could.

Dave wasn't taking advantage of me. Some people judge Dave for working his wife, but it's not that way at all. He always treated me as an equal. He thought I might consider it an insult if he had somebody come over and help me, because he would be saying, in effect, "You can't handle this." But he doesn't say that. He lets me handle things. And I treat him the same way. He can handle the domestic[8] chores.

The kids were determined not to be dudes, and they never were. They were tough pioneers. They rode horses to school. The schoolhouse is eight miles away by the road or five miles across the hills. You wouldn't believe the weather those kids took off in. Every morning they'd saddle up, get into the cow trail, and ride single file over the hill, still sort of sleepy and mesmerized.[9]

Our daughter had a wreck coming home from school when she was nine years old. The kids got in

---

[8] domestic: household
[9] mesmerized: dazed

a fight and split up, and she came home a different way. She saw some cows that were out and decided to move them back into the right pasture. Her horse fell into a coulee[10] and threw her up against the bank. When he climbed out, he stepped on her chest and his hoof hit her eye. She had a compound skull fracture and lost the eye.

She rode home. She crawled off and opened two gates on the way. She even closed them after she went through. When she arrived at the barn she fell off her horse. Her head was swollen and there was blood everywhere. You couldn't recognize her.

Dave was in Pendleton roping, so I called Big Horn Airways. We had a telephone by that time. They picked us up and took us to Sheridan. The hospital sent us right to Billings. She was in surgery there for a long time and in intensive care for a couple of weeks, but she was all right. She had no brain damage. We were so lucky.

I was really strong through all this and I stood up to it until it was all over and she was home. Then one day, after she went back to school, I really broke down and fell apart. You know, for a while you're so glad that somebody's alive that you don't worry about the cosmetic part of it, or the loss of her eye. Suddenly all that sunk in. But Dave really snapped me to. He said, "Now look, Linen. You've got a healthy, normal, wonderful daughter, and you can make her into a cripple by the way you treat her." He was absolutely right. She has done really well with it all along.

The accident upset me but it didn't make me doubt my decision to move out here. My parents had always worried about how far away from a doctor we

---

[10]coulee: deep ditch formed by running water

are. Well, I think you can get from here to Sheridan and then to Billings faster than you could get treated in a crowded emergency room in New York City. I mean, you can get *lost* in an emergency room. It just didn't take that long.

Dave and I worked side by side and I learned about ranching. In time I found that I could handle most everything here. My confidence started coming when I could recognize areas of our business that Dave was less enthusiastic about than I was. Calving heifers[11] was one of those areas.

Dave hates calving heifers, but I love it. It makes me feel so important, and I just love to feel the life come into those calves. I get very involved spiritually and physically in the whole schmeer[12] and I'm terribly conscientious.[13] Overly conscientious, really. Dave kids me about it. He says, "Now, are you sure your babies are going to be all right?" But he could see how conscientious I was and gradually he turned more and more of it over to me. Now the heifers are my department and I'm very confident with them.

We usually calve out about sixty heifers, which isn't very many, but it's the right number for me because I really get to know each one. I talk to them when they're calving. I say, "Come on Momma, push a little harder." Dave, on the other hand, is gruff and says, "Come on, you dirty son of a bitch." I say, "Dave, you can't talk to them that way. If you'd been through this, you'd know how much you can't talk to them that way." I think women have a real advantage in that department, particularly if they've had children.

---

[11]calving heifers: assisting in the birth of calves
[12]schmeer: thing
[13]conscientious: thorough

They are my family in the spring. I really get a thrill out of calving them, and then when we turn them out in the lot, the calves all run around with their tails straight over their backs, charging here and charging there. It really tickles me. I go down there and watch them for hours, and I sketch them a lot.

The other thing I really like to do is winter the yearlings.[14] When I had kids in high school, I had to live in town during the winter so they could go to school. We have a small place in there that puts up enough hay to winter about two hundred and fifty yearlings, and I took care of them.

I had an old 'fifty-nine GMC four-wheel drive named Brutus. I'd load Brutus every night and then about seven o'clock each morning Brutus and I would head for the feed ground. My dog would gather the cows and then I'd put Brutus in compound and get in the back and feed the bales. I'd turn Brutus loose, and it looked just like somebody was driving him. He'd drive himself in a snake pattern. He'd head one way until he hit a bump and then he'd head another way. Sometimes he'd head right for a snow-drift and I'd have to jump off and straighten him out or he'd bury himself. I'd have little competitions from day to day. Getting off twice and straightening him out was a really good day. Every once in a while I could feed the whole forty or forty-five bales without getting off. But sometimes Brutus was ornery[15] and I'd have to jump off five or six times.

The first year, the calves got pneumonia and I had a lot of doctoring to do. I spent a lot of time just observing the cattle—the way they walked, lay down,

---

[14]winter the yearlings: take care of newborn calves over the winter

[15]ornery: mean

held their heads and ears. I got to where I could spot when they were getting sick before they were really bad. This turned out to be the key to wintering calves and in six years we only lost three calves.

This ranch is something we all do together, and that is really different than the way I was raised. There was always the proverbial joke back East— "What would you do if your husband came home for lunch?" But we live and work together day in and day out, and we respect each other's competency in different areas. Dave is so much better at doing some parts of the ranching than I am. I don't think I'm *better* at any of it than he is, but I like to do some things that he doesn't and won't take as much time with.

Our kids work right with us, too, and I feel that the life offered on a ranch does a lot for the children as well as for the parents. Sometimes you lose patience with your loved ones before you would with an outsider. But you learn to recognize each other's limits and strengths and work around those. And you learn to respect each other for what you can do.

A lot of families are only together for recreation, and sometimes it's hard to have fun playing together. I look at people stuffed in station wagons, a thousand miles from home, broken down with a flat tire. The kids are hot and their popsicles are melting all over the back seat. I wonder how that could possibly be fun. I think you learn a lot more respect for one another working together than you do playing together.

Rose Del Castillo Guilbault spent several summers working with a group of migrant workers who came to her town. At first, she wished she had a different job. But then her attitude changed.

Hispanic, USA: The Conveyor Belt Ladies

In *The San Francisco Chronicle*
Rose Del Castillo Guilbault

The conveyor-belt ladies were the migrant women, mostly from Texas, I worked with during the summers of my teenage years. I call them conveyor-belt ladies because our entire relationship took place while sorting tomatoes on a conveyor belt.[1]

We were like a cast in a play where all the action occurs on one set. We'd return day after day to perform the same roles, only this stage was a vegetable-packing shed, and at the end of the season there was no applause. The players could look forward only to the same uninspiring[2] parts on a string of grim real-life stages.

The women and their families arrived in May for the carrot season, spent the summer in the tomato sheds and stayed through October for the bean harvest. After that, they emptied the town, some returning to their homes in Texas (cities like McAllen,

---

[1] conveyor belt: a machine that moves material through a factory or warehouse
[2] uninspiring: unable to excite enthusiasm

Douglas, Brownsville), while others continued on the migrant trail, picking cotton in the San Joaquin Valley[3] or grapefruits and oranges in the Imperial Valley.[4]

Most of these women had started in the fields. The vegetable-packing sheds were a step up, easier than the back-breaking, grueling[5] work the field demanded. The work was more tedious[6] than strenuous,[7] paid better, provided fairly steady hours and clean bathrooms. Best of all, you weren't subjected to the elements.[8]

The summer I was 16, my mother got jobs for both of us as tomato sorters. That's how I came to be included in the season sorority[9] of the conveyor belt.

The work consisted of standing and picking flawed tomatoes off the conveyor belt before they rolled off into the shipping boxes at the end of the line. These boxes were immediately loaded onto waiting delivery trucks, so it was crucial[10] not to let imperfect tomatoes through.

The work could be slow or intense, depending on the quality of the tomatoes and how many there were. Work increased when the company's deliveries got backlogged[11] or after rainy weather had delayed picking.

During those times, it was not unusual to work from 7 A.M. to midnight, playing catch-up. I never

---

[3]San Joaquin Valley: California farming community
[4]Imperial Valley: California farming community
[5]grueling: exhausting
[6]tedious: boring
[7]strenuous: physically demanding
[8]elements: bad weather
[9]sorority: female club
[10]crucial: very important
[11]backlogged: delayed

heard anyone complain about the overtime. Overtime meant desperately needed extra money.

I was not happy to be part of the agricultural work force. I would have preferred working in a dress shop or baby-sitting, like my friends. But I had a dream that would cost a lot of money—college. And the fact was, this was the highest-paying work I could do.

But it wasn't so much the work that bothered me. I was embarrassed because only Mexicans worked at packing sheds. I had heard my school-mates joke about the "ugly, fat Mexican women" at the sheds. They ridiculed[12] the way they dressed and laughed at the "funny way" they talked. I feared working with them would irrevocably[13] stigmatize[14] me, setting me further apart from my Anglo class-mates.

At 16 I was more American than Mexican and, with adolescent arrogance, felt superior to these "uneducated" women. I might be one of them, I rea-soned, but I was not like them.

But it was difficult not to like the women. They were a gregarious,[15] entertaining group, easing the long, monotonous[16] hours with bawdy[17] humor, spicy gossip and inventive laments.[18] They poked fun at all the male workers and did hysterical impersonations of a dyspeptic[19] Anglo supervisor. Although he didn't speak Spanish (other than "*Mujeres, trabajo, trabajo!*" Women, work, work!), he seemed to sense he was

---

[12]ridiculed: made fun of

[13]irrevocably: irreversibly

[14]stigmatize: give one a bad reputation

[15]gregarious: talkative

[16]monotonous: dull

[17]bawdy: coarse or vulgar; dirty

[18]inventive laments: original ways of complaining

[19]dyspeptic: having poor digestion

being laughed at. That would account for the sudden rages when he would stamp his foot and forbid us to talk until break time.

"I bet he understands Spanish and just pretends so he can hear what we say," I whispered to Rosa.

"*Ay, no, hija*,[20] it's all the buzzing in his ears that alerts him that these *viejas* (old women) are bad-mouthing him!" Rosa giggled.

But it would have been easier to tie the women's tongues in a knot than to keep them quiet. Eventually the ladies had their way and their fun, and the men learned to ignore them.

We were often shifted around, another strategy to keep us quiet. This gave me ample[21] opportunity to get to know everyone, listen to their life stories and absorb the gossip.

Pretty Rosa described her romances and her impending[22] wedding to a handsome field worker. Bertha, a heavy-set, dark-skinned woman, told me that Rosa's marriage would cause nothing but headaches because the man was younger and too handsome. Maria, large, moon-faced and placid,[23] described the births of each of her nine children, warning me about the horrors of childbirth. Pragmatic[24] Minnie, a tiny woman who always wore printed cotton dresses, scoffed at[25] Maria's stupidity, telling me she wouldn't have so many kids if she had ignored that good-for-nothing priest and gotten her tubes tied!

In unexpected moments, they could turn melancholic: recounting the babies who died because their

---

[20] *hija*: daughter; young friend
[21] ample: plenty of
[22] impending: upcoming
[23] placid: calm
[24] pragmatic: practical
[25] scoffed at: made fun of

mothers couldn't afford medical care; the alcoholic, abusive husbands who were their "cross to bear"; the racism they experienced in Texas, where they were branded "dirty Mexicans" or "Mexican dogs" and not allowed in certain restaurants.

They spoke with the detached fatalism[26] of people with limited choices and alternatives. Their lives were as raw and brutal as ghetto streets—something they accepted with an odd grace and resignation.[27]

I was appalled[28] and deeply affected by these confidences. The injustices they endured enraged me; their personal struggles overwhelmed me. I knew I could do little but sympathize.

My mother, no stranger to suffering, suggested I was too impressionable when I emotionally told her the women's stories. "That's nothing," she'd say lightly. "If they were in Mexico, life would be even harder. At least there's opportunities here, you can work."

My icy arrogance quickly thawed, that first summer, as my respect for the conveyor-belt ladies grew.

I worked in the packing sheds for several summers. The last season also turned out to be the last time I lived at home. It was the end of a chapter in my life, but I didn't know it then. I had just finished junior college and was transferring to the university. I was already over-educated for seasonal work, but if you counted the overtime, no other jobs came close to paying so well, so I went back one last time.

The ladies treated me with warmth and respect. I was a college student, deserving of special treatment.

---

[26] fatalism: belief that one's future is controlled by fate
[27] resignation: acceptance
[28] appalled: deeply upset

Aguedita, the crew chief, moved me to softer and better-paying jobs within the plant. I went from the conveyor belt to shoving boxes down a chute and finally to weighing boxes of tomatoes on a scale—the highest-paying position for a woman.

When the union's dues collector showed up, the women hid me in the bathroom. They had decided it was unfair for me to have to join the union and pay dues, since I worked only during the summer.

"Where's the student?" the union rep would ask, opening the door to a barrage of complaints about the union's unfairness.

Maria (of the nine children) tried to feed me all summer, bringing extra tortillas, which were delicious. I accepted them guiltily, always wondering if I was taking food away from her children. Others would bring rental contracts or other documents for me to explain and translate.

The last day of work was splendidly beautiful, warm and sunny. If this had been a movie, these last scenes would have been shot in soft focus, with a crescendo of music in the background.

But real life is anti-climactic.[29] As it was, nothing unusual happened. The conveyor belt's loud humming was turned off, silenced for the season. The women sighed as they removed their aprons. Some of them just walked off, calling *"Hasta la próxima!"* Until next time!

But most of the conveyor-belt ladies shook my hand, gave me a blessing or a big hug.

"Make us proud!" they said.

I hope I have.

---

[29] anti-climactic: without drama

*Richard Rodriguez was born in Califor-
nia to parents who had recently come to
the United States from Mexico. Though
he at first had trouble learning English,
he eventually mastered the language,
did very well in school, and went on to
become a college professor. Rodriguez
writes with great feeling about how his
education and success sometimes tore
him away from his roots. In the following piece, he describes an experience he
had as a college student while working
with a crew of laborers during summer
vacation.*

from Workers

In *Hunger of Memory*
Richard Rodriguez

On two occasions, the contractor hired a group of
Mexican aliens. They were employed to cut down
some trees and haul off debris.[1] In all, there were six
men of varying age. The youngest in his late
twenties; the oldest (his father?) perhaps sixty years
old. They came and they left in a single old truck.
Anonymous[2] men. They were never introduced to the
other men at the site.[3] Immediately upon their arrival,
they would follow the contractor's directions, start
working—rarely resting—seemingly driven by a
fatalistic[4] sense that work which had to be done was
best done as quickly as possible.

---

[1] debris: unwanted remains
[2] anonymous: unknown
[3] site: construction area
[4] fatalistic: belief that one has no control over one's life

I watched them sometimes. Perhaps they watched me. The only time I saw them pay me much notice was one day at lunchtime when I was laughing with the other men. The Mexicans sat apart when they ate, just as they worked by themselves. Quiet. I rarely heard them say much to each other. All I could hear were their voices calling out sharply to one another, giving directions. Otherwise, when they stood briefly resting, they talked among themselves in voices too hard to overhear.

The contractor knew enough Spanish, and the Mexicans—or at least the oldest of them, their spokesman—seemed to know enough English to communicate. But because I was around, the contractor decided one day to make me his translator. (He assumed I could speak Spanish.) I did what I was told. Shyly I went over to tell the Mexicans that the *patrón*[5] wanted them to do something else before they left for the day. As I started to speak, I was afraid with my old fear that I would be unable to pronounce the Spanish words. But it was a simple instruction I had to convey. I could say it in phrases.

The dark sweating faces turned toward me as I spoke. They stopped their work to hear me. Each nodded in response. I stood there. I wanted to say something more. But what could I say in Spanish, even if I could have pronounced the words right? Perhaps I just wanted to engage them in small talk, to be assured of their confidence, our familiarity. I thought for a moment to ask them where in Mexico they were from. Something like that. And maybe I wanted to tell them (a lie, if need be) that my parents were from the same part of Mexico.

I stood there.

---

[5] *patrón*: boss

Their faces watched me. The eyes of the man directly in front of me moved slowly over my shoulder, and I turned to follow his glance toward *el patrón* some distance away. For a moment I felt swept up by that glance into the Mexicans' company. But then I heard one of them returning to work. And then the others went back to work. I left them without saying anything more.

When they had finished, the contractor went over to pay them in cash. (He later told me that he paid them collectively[6]—'for the job,' though he wouldn't tell me their wages. He said something quickly about the good rate of exchange[7] 'in their own country.') I can still hear the loudly confident voice he used with the Mexicans. It was the sound of the *gringo*[8] I had heard as a very young boy. And I can still hear the quiet, indistinct sounds of the Mexican, the oldest, who replied. At hearing that voice I was sad for the Mexicans. Depressed by their vulnerability.[9] Angry at myself. The adventure of the summer seemed suddenly ludicrous.[10] I would not shorten the distance I felt from *los pobres*[11] with a few weeks of physical labor. I would not become like them. They were different from me.

---

[6]collectively: as a group
[7]rate of exchange: rate at which U.S. dollars are exchanged into foreign dollars
[8]*gringo*: foreigner, especially an American
[9]vulnerability: openness to harm
[10]ludicrous: ridiculous
[11]*los pobres*: the poor

REFLECT ·

What is John Coleman's attitude toward blue-collar, or "laborer," jobs in "Wednesday, February 28"? Do you think most Americans agree with him? Why do you feel as you do?

How does Linen Bliss feel about life on the ranch?

What new talents and skills did Bliss discover within herself as a result of living on a ranch?

How did Rose Del Castillo Guilbault ("Hispanic, USA: The Conveyor Belt Ladies") feel at first about working with the migrant women? How did she feel by the time she quit work for college? What made her change her mind?

How did Richard Rodriguez ("Workers") feel when he talked to the Mexican aliens for his boss? Why did he feel this way?

Contrast Guilbault's and Rodriguez's experiences working summer jobs. Why do you think they had different experiences in similar situations?

WRITE ·

If you could trade places for a day with anyone else on earth, who would it be? Why?

What do you think Linen's family and friends in the East thought when she decided to marry Dave Bliss and live on his ranch in Montana? Imagine you are related to her, and write her a letter.

Imagine that you are one of the people in this unit and have been invited to give a brief speech to a class of adult students. Write a short speech explaining why you traded one life for another and what you think you learned.

A lack of money, guidance, and education has left some of our children without hope for the future. This young man's face is a study in anger and despair.

SHORT LIVES, HARD LIVES

Do you know—or can you imagine—what it's like to live where violence and death occur almost daily? How does it feel to know that the streets where you walk and playgrounds where you play are dangerous? Too many of our neighborhoods have become deadly places. Too many of our children have lost hope of finding a better life.

We hear and see so many reports about violence that we are sometimes in danger of becoming used to it. It's all too easy to turn our backs and look the other way. It's all too easy to pretend that violence is someone else's problem.

The readings in this unit show, close up, the toll that hopelessness and violence can take. As you read each selection, think about how you would feel if the people were your family, friends, or neighbors. Are there ways for people and neighborhoods to be saved—or to save themselves?

Mitch Albom is a popular sportswriter for the Detroit Free Press. *Below, he writes about Damon Bailes, a young man who was shot during a pickup basketball game. Bailes's story is repeated nearly every day in cities across the United States. As Albom's title suggests, street violence is an American tragedy.*

from *A Tragedy Too Easy to Ignore*

In *Best American Sports Writing 1993*
Mitch Albom

"We got next!"

It was a warm May night and the basketball game was moving up and down the asphalt.

"We got next!" The kids were sweating as they waited. They dribbled in place. Damon, whose nickname was "Smooth," looked around. He had never been to this court before, outside old Bentley High in Livonia. He and four friends, Lawrence Poole, Torrin Cottrell, Kevin Franklin and Terril Malone, had started the afternoon in the city, but they lost their first game, and the line was too long to wait for another. There are not enough playable courts in Detroit. And far too many kids with time on their hands.

Poole said he knew a place in the suburbs where the competition was pretty good. So they got in the car and drove to Livonia. Five black kids in a Ford Escort. They were not there long before a police car stopped them.

"Your plates are expired," the officer said. When he ran their names through the computer, one of them, Kevin Franklin, was shown as delinquent[1] on child support payments. He was arrested and taken to jail.

"Let's just go home." Torrin said.

They almost did. But Damon wanted to play ball, and Poole did, too. So now they stood under the floodlights at Bentley, four city kids, waiting for the suburban rims.

"Check the guy in the red shorts," Poole said to Damon as they watched the game.

"Uh-huh."

"There go the shorts we want, the long kind."

"Yeah, they nice. We should buy some of those."

That was it, they claim. Nothing more. The guy in the red shorts, Tyrone Swint, also from Detroit, might have seen them looking and pointing. He would later tell police he thought Damon was "a guy who jumped me" at a Detroit nightclub. Whatever. Something set him off.

And he had a gun.

"Bring the car around," he told a friend.

"What for?"

"We might have a fight."

The suburbs were about to meet the city.

"O.K., let's play," Torrin said, and he bounced an inbounds pass. They ran up and down the court several times. Damon, a six-foot-two, baby-faced guard who had dropped out of high school but starred in church leagues and was hoping to get to a small college if he could pass his equivalency exams, tossed in a couple baskets. Now he dribbled the ball upcourt. He loved this part of the game, when everything was open, everyone was moving, and he was in control. He felt special. Maybe this was the only place he ever felt special.

---

[1]delinquent: late

He was about to make a pass to his best friend, Poole. Suddenly, witnesses say, Tyrone Swint, the guy in the red shorts, came up behind Damon and pulled out a gun. He shot Damon in the back of the head. This was before anyone had a chance to yell, "Look out!" This was while Damon was dribbling a basketball. The bullet went through Damon's brain and lodged between the skull and the skin. He went down. The ball rolled away.

"Everyone started running," Cottrell says. "I saw the guy shoot Damon and then he shot again at someone else. As I was running, I saw him go jumping into the window of this black car and they drove away."

The black car was the escape horse, and Tyrone and his buddy were cowboys heading out of town. They drove down Five Mile Road and turned onto Middlebelt. Tyrone threw his gun out the window. It landed in the dirt. Later, Tyrone jumped out of the car and ran through the streets alone.

Back on the court, under the suburban floodlights, Damon Bailes was lying in blood. One of the players was trying to take his pulse. Poole was yelling at the oncoming EMS[2] workers: "My boy's lying here shot! He's shot!"

Torrin was crying. He had known Damon since they were kids. They played in church leagues together. The summer before they had gone to Saginaw for an all-day tournament, and they won the whole thing and everyone got trophies. On the bus ride home, Damon was laughing and talking about how good they were. He had scored all these points. They waved their trophies at each other.

Now Damon was flat, not moving, his head was swollen and bloody, and there was a big knot on the

---

[2]EMS: emergency medical service

forehead where he had hit the pavement. Torrin and Poole couldn't stop crying. They were still kids, really. They had never been in trouble like this. They ran to the school and found a pay phone. They called Damon's aunt.

"Damon been shot!" Poole said. "Damon been shot!"

Inside the quiet A-frame house on Greenlawn in Detroit there is a small, white, plastic Christmas tree. Velma Bailes, Damon's mother, a woman who looks too young for nine children, no husband, and an ominous[3] pile of hospital bills, bought the tree last year, at Shoppers World, for $25.99. She walks around its needles, and says Damon wants a small TV for Christmas, so he can watch programs from his bed.

"Will he get what he wants?"

"He'll get what he needs."

"What does he need?"

"He needs boots for the snow."

It has been seven months since the bullet, which was taken from Damon's brain and given to the police. Damon was in a coma for the first five weeks. Velma would try to talk to him in the hospital, as the doctors had suggested.

"Damon, we need you to come back," she would say. She would hold his hand and look at the tubes in his throat, nose and arms. She would go home.

One night, a nurse called and said to come down quickly. The patient next to Damon was saying, "Damon can't see!"

"How do you know?"

"He woke up yellin', 'I can't see!' "

The bullet had hit the lobe that controls vision. It also had left Damon paralyzed on the right side. In

---

[3] ominous: hinting at trouble to come

the months that followed he would regain a slurred speech, partial[4] vision and some feeling in his otherwise dead right leg and arm. The vision bothered him most. He would cry for hours over his near-blindness.

"He was always saying, 'How can I play basketball if I can't see?' " recalls Mary Roy, who manages the brain-injury program at the Rehabilitation Institute of Michigan. "We tried to tell him, 'Damon, there are other things you can do that are more important than basketball.' "

This, of course, is wishful thinking. The truth is, for a kid like Damon, there was only basketball. He was never college material. He couldn't get through two different high schools. He never held a job. He lived at home, he had a baby with his girlfriend. Maybe he foolishly figured that little leather ball would someday lift him up above all this, the welfare checks, the food stamps, the porch that is falling apart.

If he was stupid, so be it. He is not the first. But he did no wrong. He committed no crimes. The tendency[5] in well-to-do circles is to dismiss a kid such as Damon as hopeless, destined to a bad finish, as if this were some kind of birthright as an urban baby. But if we think like that, we cut the veins out of our city and, don't kid yourself, our suburbs, too. Young black males. Wounded by gunshot. Young black males. Killed by gunshot. This is all our story. This is where we live. Detroit. A place where, this year alone, 266 children under the age of seventeen have been shot.

We are dying, one bullet at a time.

---

[4]partial: some but not all
[5]tendency: trend

The short pieces that follow were written during a school year by sixth-graders in an inner-city New Jersey school. The students' writings were collected and published by their teacher. As you read, recall what life was like when you were ten or eleven years old. How do your memories of childhood compare with what these children's lives are like?

Children's Fears

From *Voices of City Children*
Nicholas Duva

THE KNIFE
There was this knife,
It stopped a life.
It let his blood flow,
And his life go.
I saw this Saturday.

RIOT
It started on a Sunday
morning. There was a lot of people
starting a fight with other people
in the bar.
People were killed, and
blood was all over the street.
Houses were burned,
Cars were stolen.
I was feeling bad for the babys.

JUST NEXT DOOR

This lady, she lived just next door to me. She was asleep in the dark. At night, someone came to her house to rape and kill her. This happened to her once before. She be so scared, she went crazy. And so the lady jumped from the 3 floor window and died.

That is why you sure better keep your lights on.

WHY I'M AFRAID

One night when I was going on an errand to get chinese food I went down this dark street. There I saw rats, cats, dogs, and lots of crazy people around. This one man he came to me and he said are you going somewhere down the street. I said yes. He said that I wouldn't if I were you. I said why, but he didn't say anything, he just walked away.

So I stood there saying should I or shouldn't I. I went down the street, and I saw a dead man laying in the street, and another man was coming at me with blood on his hands and his face. I ran and I ran and I ran until I got home and at my house they said where's the chinese food.

Anna Quindlen is a widely read newspaper columnist. She writes about events in her life and in the daily news. In the following piece, Quindlen reflects on the story of two teenagers who were killed in the hallway of their high school by another student.

The quotation that begins this piece is from the story of Peter Pan. In the story, the "lost boys" go off to Neverland, where they have wonderful adventures and never grow old. Quindlen makes a grim comparison to the lost boys of our inner cities. They never grow up either. They die.

To Defray Expenses[1]

From *Thinking Out Loud*
Anna Quindlen

"They are the children who fall out of their perambulators[2] when the nurse is looking the other way. If they are not claimed in seven days they are sent far away to the Neverland to defray expenses."

The Lost Boys made news. The television crews and the newspaper reporters went to that Neverland called East New York to take note of the fact that one of them, aged fifteen, had allegedly[3] shot and killed

---

[1]to defray expenses: help pay for the cost of
[2]perambulators: baby carriages
[3]allegedly: reportedly

two others in a high school hallway in what class-mates called a "beef." This means a disagreement.

It could have been Bushwick or the South Bronx or any of the other New York neighborhoods that are shorthand for going nowhere. It could have been Chicago or L.A. or any one of dozens of other cities. The Lost Boys are everywhere. Most especially in prison. By then, unlike the children Peter Pan described, they have grown up.

We reporters won't stay long. The Lost Boys claim public attention for only a short time, and many of us are loath[4] to walk in their neighborhoods, which makes us no different from the people who live in them. The mayor was at the high school the day of the killings. He came to tell the students that they, too, could build a future. For many of them, the future is that short period of time between today and the moment when they shoot or get shot.

Homicide[5] is the leading cause of death for black teenagers in America.

There is a lot of talk now about metal detectors and gun control. Both are good things. But they are no more a solution than forks and spoons are a solution to world hunger. Kids, particularly kids who live amid crack houses and abandoned buildings, have a right to think of their school as a safe haven.[6] But it's important to remember that a kid can get himself a box cutter and wait outside until the last bell rings. With a metal detector, you can keep the homicide out of the hallways. Perhaps with something more, you can keep the homicide out of the heart.

---

[4] loath: very unwilling
[5] homicide: murder
[6] haven: place free of harm or danger

"These boys die like it's nothing," said Angela Burton, whose boyfriend was one of the two killed in East New York.

The problem is that when we look into this abyss,[7] it goes so deep that we get dizzy and pull back from the edge. Teenage mothers. Child abuse. Crowded schools. Homes without fathers. Projects lousy with drugs, vermin,[8] crime. And, always, the smell of urine in the elevator. I have never been in a project that hasn't had that odor, and I have never smelled it without wondering, If your home smells like a bathroom, what does that tell you about yourself?

One of the ways to motivate kids is to say that if you do this bad thing now, you won't be able to do this good thing tomorrow. That doesn't work with the Lost Boys. They stopped believing in tomorrow a long time ago. The impulse control of an adolescent, the conviction[9] that sooner or later you'll end up dead or in jail anyhow, and a handgun you can buy on the corner easier than getting yourself a pair of new Nikes: the end result is preordained.[10]

"If you don't got a gun, you got to get one," said one teenager hanging with his friends at the corner of East New York and Pennsylvania avenues.

If news is sometimes defined as aberration,[11] as Man Bites Dog, it's the successes we should be rushing out to cover in these neighborhoods, the kids who graduate, who get jobs, who stay clean. Dr. Alwyn Cohall, a pediatrician who runs four school-based clinics in New York, remembers the day he was

---

[7]abyss: bottomless hole
[8]vermin: hateful pests such as rats and cockroaches
[9]conviction: belief
[10]preordained: decided in advance
[11]aberration: something unusual or abnormal

giving one of those kids a college physical, which is the happiest thing he ever does, when from outside he heard the sound. Pow. Pow. One moment he was filling out the forms for a future, the next giving CPR[12] to another teenager with a gunshot wound blossoming in his chest. The kid died on the cement.

"He never even made the papers next day," the doctor recalled.

The story in East New York will likely end with the funerals. A fifteen-year-old killer is not that unusual; many city emergency rooms provide coloring books on gun safety. Dr. Cohall says that when the students at his schools come back after the long hot summer, they are routinely asked by the clinic staff how many of their friends were shot over vacation. The good doctor knows that it is possible to reclaim some of the Lost Boys, but it requires money, dedication, and, above all, the will to do it. Or we can continue to let them go. To defray expenses.

---

[12]CPR: cardiopulmonary resuscitation; procedure designed to restore a normal heartbeat to someone in distress

Latoya Hunter and her family moved from Jamaica to New York City when she was still a child. When Hunter entered junior high, she began keeping a diary in the form of letters to an imaginary friend named Janice.

January 9, 1991

From *The Diary of Latoya Hunter*
Latoya Hunter

Dear Janice,

Today gunshots echo in my head. They are the same gunshots that killed an innocent human being right across from my house last night. They are the same gunshots that have scarred me, I think, forever.

Late last night, I was in bed when I heard a man screaming for a police officer. I told myself, I didn't hear that. Later I told myself I didn't hear the four gunshots that followed his cry for help. I lay there in bed and it was like I was frozen. I didn't want to move an inch. I then heard hysterical crying. I ran to the window when I couldn't keep myself back any longer. What I saw outside were cops arriving. I ran into my parent's room and woke them up. By that time, tears were pouring unstoppably from my eyes. I couldn't stop shaking. My parents looked through the window and got dressed. They rushed outside and I followed them. It turned out that I knew the person who got shot. He worked at the store at the corner. He was always so nice to me, he was always smiling. He didn't know much English but we still managed a friendship.

I can't believe this happened. Things like this happen everyday in N.Y., but not in my neighborhood, not to people I know.

Gary Soto is a well-known Mexican-American author who often writes about growing up in southern California.

"Fear" is a little different from the other pieces in this unit. It focuses on the bully's emotions as well as his victim's. By the time you finish reading, you may wonder who the victim really is.

Fear

From *Living Up the Street*
Gary Soto

A cold day after school. Frankie T., who would drown his brother by accident that coming spring and would use a length of pipe to beat a woman in a burglary years later, had me pinned on the ground behind a backstop, his breath sour as meat left out in the sun. "*Cabron*,"[1] he called me and I didn't say anything. I stared at his face, shaped like the sole of a shoe, and just went along with the insults, although now and then I tried to raise a shoulder in a halfhearted[2] struggle because that was part of the game.

He let his drool yo-yo from his lips, missing my feet by only inches, after which he giggled and called me names. Finally he let me up. I slapped grass from my jacket and pants, and pulled my shirt tail from my pants to shake out the fistful of dirt he had stuffed in my collar. I stood by him, nervous and red-faced from struggling, and when he suggested that we climb the monkey bars together, I followed him

---

[1] *cabron*: fool
[2] halfhearted: unenthusiastic

quietly to the kid's section of Jefferson Elementary. He climbed first, with small grunts, and for a second I thought of running but knew he would probably catch me—if not then, the next day. There was no way out of being a fifth grader—the daily event of running to teachers to show them your bloody nose. It was just a fact, like having lunch.

So I climbed the bars and tried to make conversation, first about the girls in our classroom and then about kickball. He looked at me smiling as if I had a camera in my hand, his teeth green like the underside of a rock, before he relaxed his grin into a simple gray line across his face. He told me to shut up. He gave me a hard stare and I looked away to a woman teacher walking to her car and wanted very badly to yell for help. She unlocked her door, got in, played with her face in the visor mirror while the engine warmed, and then drove off with blue smoke trailing. Frankie was watching me all along and when I turned to him, he laughed, "*Chale!*[3] She can't help you, *ese*."[4] He moved closer to me on the bars and I thought he was going to hit me; instead he put his arm around my shoulder, squeezing firmly in friendship. "C'mon, chicken, let's be cool."

I opened my mouth and tried to feel happy as he told me what he was going to have for Thanksgiving. "My Mamma's got a turkey and ham, lots of potatoes, yams and stuff like that. I saw it in the refrigerator. And she says we gonna get some pies. Really, *ese*."

Poor liar, I thought, smiling as we clunked our heads softly like good friends. He had seen the same afternoon program on TV as I had, one in which a woman in an apron demonstrated how to prepare a Thanksgiving dinner. I knew he would have tortillas

---

[3] *chale*: chicken; coward
[4] *ese*: pal; brother

and beans, a round steak maybe, and oranges from his backyard. He went on describing his Thanksgiving, then changed over to Christmas—the new bicycle, the clothes, the G.I. Joes.[5] I told him that it sounded swell, even though I knew he was making it all up. His mother would in fact stand in line at the Salvation Army[6] to come away hugging armfuls of toys that had been tapped back into shape by reformed alcoholics with veined noses. I pretended to be excited and asked if I could come over to his place to play after Christmas. "Oh, yeah, anytime," he said, squeezing my shoulder and clunking his head against mine.

When he asked what I was having for Thanksgiving, I told him that we would probably have a ham with pineapple on the top. My family was slightly better off than Frankie's, though I sometimes walked around with cardboard in my shoes and socks with holes big enough to be ski masks, so holidays were extravagant happenings. I told him about the scalloped potatoes, the candied yams, the frozen green beans, and the pumpkin pie.

His eyes moved across my face as if he were deciding where to hit me—nose, temple, chin, talking mouth—and then he lifted his arm from my shoulder and jumped from the monkey bars, grunting as he landed. He wiped sand from his knees while looking up and warned me not to mess around with him any more. He stared with such a great meanness that I had to look away. He warned me again and then walked away. Incredibly relieved, I jumped from the bars and ran looking over my shoulder until I turned onto my street.

---

[5] G.I. Joes: soldier dolls
[6] Salvation Army: charity that raises money by repairing and reselling old clothes, toys, and other items

Frankie scared most of the school out of its wits and even had girls scampering out of view when he showed himself on the playground. If he caught us without notice, we grew quiet and stared down at our shoes until he passed after a threat or two. If he pushed us down, we stayed on the ground with our eyes closed and pretended that we were badly hurt. If he riffled[7] through our lunch bags, we didn't say anything. He took what he wanted, after which we sighed and watched him walk away peeling an orange or chewing big chunks of an apple.

Still, that afternoon when he called Mr. Koligian, our teacher, a foul name—we grew scared for him. Mr. Koligian pulled and tugged at his body until it was in his arms and then out of his arms as he hurled Frankie against the building. Some of us looked away because it was unfair. We knew the house he lived in: The empty refrigerator, the father gone, the mother in a sad bathrobe, the beatings, the yearnings[8] for something to love. When the teacher manhandled[9] him, we all wanted to run away, but instead we stared and felt shamed. Robert, Adele, Yolanda shamed; Danny, Alfonso, Brenda shamed; Nash, Margie, Rocha shamed. We all watched him flop about as Mr. Koligian shook and grew red from anger. We knew his house and, for some, it was the same one to walk home to: The broken mother, the indifferent[10] walls, the refrigerator's glare which fed the people no one wanted.

---

[7] riffled: quickly looked
[8] yearnings: desires
[9] manhandled: handled roughly
[10] indifferent: uncaring

REFLECT ·······································

How does Mitch Albom, the author of "A Tragedy Too Easy to Ignore," feel about the shooting of Damon Bailes? About Bailes himself?

What is your reaction to the pieces in "Children's Fears"? Why do you feel as you do?

What acts of violence does Anna Quindlen describe in "To Defray Expenses"?

What point is Quindlen trying to make by describing the acts?

What is Latoya Hunter's ("January 9, 1991") reaction to the shooting in her neighborhood? What does this reaction tell you about her?

As the events he describes were happening, Gary Soto's attitude toward Frankie T. ("Fear") changed. Describe the different feelings Soto had about the bully. How do you think the author feels about Frankie now? How can you tell?

In your opinion, what steps should we take to stop the violence in our neighborhoods?

WRITE ·····································

In "Fear," Gary Soto writes about a time in his childhood when he was afraid. Describe a time when someone or something frightened you.

What do you think we should do to stop the violence in our neighborhoods? Write a letter to the editor of your local newspaper telling what you think should be done.

In "To Defray Expenses," Dr. Cohall reports that a few young people escape from even the very worst surroundings and go on to make secure, successful lives for themselves. Describe what you think it takes for them to succeed. Do these people share certain characteristics or skills, or are they just lucky? Explain your reasoning.

CREDITS

Essay on pages 65–72: "The Overspill," from *I Am One of You Forever*, by Fred Chappell. Copyright © 1985 by Fred Chappell, published by Louisiana State University Press. Used with permission.

Excerpt on pages 76–78: From *Can You Trust a Tomato in January?* by Vince Staten. Copyright © 1993 by Vince Staten. Reprinted by permission of Simon & Schuster, Inc.

Article on pages 79–81: "Chewing Gum," by Don L. Wulffson. Text from "Chewing Gum," pp. 27–29 of *The Invention of Ordinary Things*, by Don L. Wulffson, illustrated by Roy Doty. Copyright © 1981 by Don L. Wulffson; illustrations, copyright © 1981 by Roy Doty. Reprinted by permission of Lothrop, Lee & Shepard books, a division of William Morrow & Company, Inc.

Article on pages 82–84: "Velcro: Improving on Nature," from *They All Laughed . . .*, by Ira Flatow. Copyright © 1992 by Ira Flatow. Reprinted by permission of HarperCollins Publishers, Inc.

Essay on pages 85–87: "Dr. Pemberton's Pick-Me-Up," from *Paul Harvey's The Rest of the Story*, by Paul Aurandt. Copyright © 1977 by Paulynne, Inc. Used by Permission of Doubleday, a division of Bantam Doubleday Dell Publishing Group, Inc.

Essay on pages 92–94: "Words in a Blue Notebook," by Eula Lee Maddox, from *Legacies*, by Maury Leibovitz and Linda Solomon. Copyright © 1993 by The Jewish Association of Services for the Aged. Reprinted by permission of HarperCollins Publishers, Inc.

Excerpt on pages 95–96: "Freedom," from *Gifts of Age: Portraits and Essays of 32 Remarkable Women*, by Charlotte Painter. Copyright © 1985, published by Chronicle Books. Reprinted by permission of Chronicle Books.

Letter on pages 97–100: From *Dear Dad*, by Louie Anderson. Copyright © 1989 by Louzelle Productions, Inc. Used by permission of Viking Penguin, a division of Penguin Books USA Inc.

Excerpt on pages 101–105: From "Me and the Guy Upstairs," by Penny Longworth, from *No More Frogs, No More Princes*. Copyright © 1993 by Joanne F. Vickers and Barbara L. Thomas. Published by The Crossing Press, Freedom, CA.

Excerpt on pages 110–112: "Wednesday, February 28," from *Blue Collar Journal*, by John R. Coleman. Copyright © 1973 by John R. Coleman. Reprinted by permission of Collier Associates.

Excerpt on pages 113–119: From "Linen Bliss," from *Cowgirls: Women of the American West*. Copyright © 1982 by Teresa Jordan. Reprinted by permission of the author.

Essay on pages 120–125: "Hispanic, USA: The Conveyor Belt Ladies," by Rose Del Castillo Guilbault, from *the San Francisco Chronicle*, "This World," April 15, 1990. Reprinted by permission of the author.